The CALVIN INSTITUTE OF CHRISTIAN WORSHIP LITURGICAL STUDIES Series, edited by John D. Witvliet, is designed to promote reflection on the history, theology, and practice of Christian worship and to stimulate worship renewal in Christian congregations. Contributions include writings by pastoral worship leaders from a wide range of communities and scholars from a wide range of disciplines. The ultimate goal of these contributions is to nurture worship practices that are spiritually vital and theologically rooted.

Published

The Pastor as Minor Poet: Texts and Subtexts in the Ministerial Life
M. Craig Barnes

Touching the Altar: The Old Testament for Christian Worship
Carol M. Bechtel, Editor

God Against Religion:
Rethinking Christian Theology through Worship
Matthew Myer Boulton

Inclusive yet Discerning: Navigating Worship Artfully
Frank Burch Brown

What Language Shall I Borrow? The Bible and Christian Worship
Ronald P. Byars

A Primer on Christian Worship:
Where We've Been, Where We Are, Where We Can Go
William Dyrness

Christian Worship Worldwide:
Expanding Horizons, Deepening Practices
Charles E. Farhadian

Gather into One: Praying and Singing Globally
C. Michael Hawn

The Substance of Things Seen:
Art, Faith, and the Christian Community
Robin M. Jensen

Our Worship
Abraham Kuyper, Edited by Harry Boonstra

Wonderful Words of Life:
Hymns in American Protestant History and Theology
Richard J. Mouw and Mark A. Noll, Editors

Discerning the Spirits:
A Guide to Thinking about Christian Worship Today
Cornelius Plantinga Jr. and Sue A. Rozeboom

Voicing God's Psalms
Calvin Seerveld

My Only Comfort:
Death, Deliverance, and Discipleship in the Music of Bach
Calvin R. Stapert

A New Song for an Old World: Musical Thought in the Early Church
Calvin R. Stapert

An Architecture of Immanence:
Architecture for Worship and Ministry Today
Mark A. Torgerson

A More Profound Alleluia: Theology and Worship in Harmony
Leanne Van Dyk, Editor

Christian Worship in Reformed Churches Past and Present
Lukas Vischer, Editor

The Biblical Psalms in Christian Worship:
A Brief Introduction and Guide to Resources
John D. Witvliet

Inclusive yet Discerning

NAVIGATING WORSHIP ARTFULLY

Frank Burch Brown

William B. Eerdmans Publishing Company

Grand Rapids, Michigan / Cambridge, U.K.

Published 2009 by
Wm. B. Eerdmans Publishing Co.
2140 Oak Industrial Drive N.E., Grand Rapids, Michigan 49505 /
P.O. Box 163, Cambridge CB3 9PU U.K.

Printed in the United States of America

14 13 12 11 10 09   7 6 5 4 3 2 1

Library of Congress Cataloging-in-Publication Data

Brown, Frank Burch, 1948-
Inclusive yet discerning: navigating worship artfully / Frank Burch Brown.
p.   cm.   — (The Calvin Institute of Christian Worship
liturgical studies series)
Includes bibliographical references.
ISBN 978-0-8028-6256-3 (pbk.: alk. paper)
1. Public worship.   2. Christianity and art.
3. Aesthetics — Religious aspects — Christianity.
4. Church music.   5. Music — Religious aspects — Christianity.
I. Title.

BV15.B75   2009
264 — dc22

2008031406

www.eerdmans.com

In memory of my mother

Jane Purser Brown

(1920-2000)

Contents

Series Preface

Many of our ideas and preferences about art, music, drama, and dance are formed apart from the life of the church and the practice of worship. Every museum, concert, studio, gallery, scholarly analysis, conference, advertisement, and published review we encounter reflects a certain set of values and assumptions about what good and bad art is, what function it plays in human life, and how we might value or appropriate it.

We then bring these assumptions with us to the public worship services we attend or plan or lead, and to the works of art and music we encounter there. At times, these assumptions may help God's people worship faithfully and vibrantly. They might, for example, help us to appreciate an artwork from a culture other than our own, or to discern the pathos or energy of a given work and its significance for Christian prayer and proclamation. At other times, however, these assumptions can erect barriers to faithful and vital worship. They might tempt us to worship artists or artworks instead of God, for example, or to fall into the kind of elitism or pragmatism that erodes our experience of grateful awe that is inherent in the act of worship. They might even prevent us from discerning how emerging forms of cultural expression might genuinely revitalize and deepen worship practices.

As several commentators in a variety of traditions have noted, one of the central problems in the worship life of churches today is precisely the fact that so many of our culturally shaped assumptions, especially those about public assemblies and works of art, go unchallenged and unrefined by the church. Our artistic experience in worship is then shaped more by the norms and values of other cultural institutions than by the norms and values intrinsic to worship. In this context, we need books like this one, books to challenge and deepen our assumptions about art, artists, taste, and worship itself.

We need, in other words, access to the rich wisdom of Christian reflection in the discipline of liturgical aesthetics, a field of inquiry that gathers insight from a variety of sources to inform and sharpen how we prepare for, experience, and reflect on the artworks in many media that shape our public worship assemblies. The sources that contribute to this discussion are manifold: devotional and scholarly biblical expositions, philosophical and theological treatises, and individual works of art, dance, drama, and music. Work in this field is an endlessly interesting and instructive task, given the explosion of liturgical expression over the span of more than three thousand years and in well over two hundred cultures.

Frank Burch Brown is an ideal tour guide into this rich and complex field. He is a rigorous theologian, a practicing church musician and composer, and a well-regarded teacher of students from many religious traditions. Further, he has been a thoughtful and discerning writer on many themes related to this book, especially in his three major earlier books.

In *Transfiguration: Poetic Metaphor and the Languages of Religious Belief* (University of North Carolina Press, 1983), Burch Brown described how the use of poetic language and theoretical or analytical language each affect each other in a reciprocal process of shaping meaning. We live by and through a dynamic dance of language that is evocative and metaphorical on the one hand, and that is denotative and discursive on the other. This motif of "transfiguration" runs compellingly throughout much of his writing, and helps him, even in this book, resist any isolated analysis of a given artwork, artist, cultural or historical context, or mode of analysis. Every example of artwork exists in multiple transformative relationships with people, objects, dispositions, and values. Any discussion of them that oversimplifies this complexity—a regular feature of many writings on liturgical artwork—often leads to unnecessary dualisms, division, and lack of discernment.

In *Religious Aesthetics* (Princeton University Press, 1993), Burch Brown charted an even more comprehensive approach to several central questions in aesthetic theory, reflecting on the complex milieu that informs all artistry and all reception of artworks, probing the complex functions of the body, mind, and soul in aesthetic experience, and justifying the importance of theological reflection on art. In a particularly memorable chapter, he describes four kinds of aesthetic sins—the Philistine, the Aesthete, the Intolerant, and the Indiscriminate—that tenaciously reside not only in every community arts organization, but also inside every church worship committee, and indeed in every one of us. The presentation of these four sins upholds a vision of a kind of "aesthetic poise" that does not respond to a given problem (e.g., an indiscriminate approach to the arts) by simply falling into another opposite and equally destructive problem (e.g., an intolerant approach).

In *Good Taste, Bad Taste, and Christian Taste: Aesthetics in Religious Life* (Oxford University Press, 2000), Burch Brown expanded his thinking on questions related to the reception and critique of works of art. He argued for a notion of "ecumenical taste," an approach that achieves the rare distinction of being discriminating, but not elitist, and of being flexible without condoning cliché or kitsch. Drawing on a host of examples in multiple artistic media from multiple centuries and cultures, he both challenges simplistic universal claims about artistic meaning and emboldens arts, critics, and the rest of us to make more discerning judgments about the artworks we encounter. Thoughtful readers become better stewards of the time, money, and energy that are rightly devoted to the arts, in all their many forms.

In the book you are now holding, Burch Brown extends many of these perspectives, harvesting fruit from these earlier lines of thought for a broad audience of those interested in vital worship practices. This book is more succinct than the others, and it focuses more exclusively on the practice of worship. It is an ideal introduction, then, to the field of liturgical aesthetics for all pastors, teachers, artists, musicians, and—indeed—for all worshipers who are eager to deepen their own love for and experience of public worship.

I would suspect that most readers will come to this book with some firm convictions or opinions about the artistic life of their own congregation. I would encourage them to write these down before they begin reading, and then to restate them, drawing on examples and themes from this book, after completing their reading. I strongly suspect that most readers will find that their second version will feature greater nuance, hospitality, and vigor than their first. I say this because of my experience of observing students and others encounter Burch Brown's work. While many authors on the arts are adept at confirming what readers already think and believe, Burch Brown is adept at sharpening, even converting his readers. Like a wise art-museum docent, he gently but firmly introduces us to a world more interesting and complex than we ever imagined and then invites us to rethink our basic assumptions. May God's Spirit challenge, teach, and inspire all who pause to study these pages, and so strengthen the church and its practice of worship.

JOHN D. WITVLIET
Calvin Institute of Christian Worship
Calvin College and
   Calvin Theological Seminary
Grand Rapids, Michigan

Permissions

A number of the chapters here appeared in slightly different form in earlier publications and are reprinted here with permission:

"Christian Music: More than Just the Words." In the series "The Medium and the Message," *Theology Today,* vol. 62, no. 2 (July 2005): 223-29.

"Enjoyment and Discernment in the Music of Worship." In *Theology Today,* vol. 58, no. 3, Issue on Worship (October 2001): 342-58.

"Is Good Art Good for Christian Worship?" was originally titled "Is Good Art Good for Religion?" In *Theological Aesthetics after von Balthasar,* ed. Oleg Bychkov and James Fodor. London: Ashgate, 2008.

"On Being Beautiful and Religious at the Same Time: Plotinus's Aesthetics for the Present." In *The Subjective Eye: Essays in Culture, Religion, and Gender,* ed. Richard Valantasis and Janet F. Carlson, a Festschrift for Margaret Miles, Princeton Theological Monograph Series 59, pp. 17-32. Eugene, Ore.: Wipf and Stock/Pickwick Publications, 2006.

"On Not Giving Short Shrift to the Arts in Liturgy: The Testimony of Pope Benedict XVI (Cardinal Ratzinger)." In *ARTS: The Arts in Religious and Theological Studies,* vol. 17, no. 1 (2005): 13-19.

"Religious Music and Secular Music: A Calvinist Perspective, Re-formed." In *Theology Today,* vol. 63, no. 1 (April 2006): 11-21.

"Singing Together (with All Creation): Dilemmas and Delights" was originally titled "How Moveable Is the Feast?" In *The Hymn: A Journal of Congregational Song,* vol. 55, no. 4 (October 2004): 8-14.

Author's Preface

It now seems long ago, although in fact only slightly over a decade has passed. The cover of the August 1996 *Atlantic Monthly* announced a Christian cultural revolution: "Giant 'full-service' churches are winning millions of 'customers' with [their] pop-culture packaging. They may also be building an important new form of community." In the corresponding interior article, author Charles Trueheart described what he called the "Next Church": No spires. No crosses. No robes. No clerical collars. No hard pews. No kneelers. No biblical gobbledygook. No rote prayer. No fire, no brimstone. No pipe organs. No dreary eighteenth-century hymns. No forced solemnity. No Sunday finery. No collection plates.[1]

The list was not meant to be complete, and allowance was made for possible asterisks and exceptions. But the meaning was plain, and became plainer in the rest of the article. Centuries of European tradition and Christian habit were deliberately being abandoned to clear the way for new, contemporary forms of worship and belonging. The

1. See my discussion (which this paragraph partly paraphrases) in *Good Taste, Bad Taste, and Christian Taste: Aesthetics in Religious Life* (New York: Oxford University Press, 2000), pp. 230-51; revised and reprinted in the *Christian Century,* September 13-20, 2000, pp. 904-11. See also related material in *Music in Christian Worship,* ed. Charlotte Kroeker (Collegeville, Minn.: Liturgical Press, 2005), pp. 135-55.

"Next Church" and its many smaller, typically suburban relatives were held up as models of the options available to Christians who wanted to "catch the next wave." And music provided the clearest indication of the revolutionary change. The musical idioms of the Next Church were current, casual, and often unapologetically entertaining.

What could make that excited report on these developments already seem somewhat dated — although it is certainly of our time — is just that the changes described there have quickly settled in and spread out, and in some places have come to seem relatively normal, though they are by no means universal. It is not that there hasn't been considerable conflict and resistance. Often the "Next Church" has broken away to become a new congregation, sometimes without any denominational identity; at other times it has required a separate worship service. Among some Christians the resistance is firmer than ever to the "Next" worship style, which typically abounds in video clips, PowerPoint presentations, pop songs, and high-tech media. Yet efforts at compromise have grown subtler and perhaps wiser. Meanwhile, an alternative "new wave" has already emerged conspicuously enough to be clearly identified. It is variously known as the "Emerging Church" or "Emergent Church," or (in still another form) as an "Emerging Christian Way."[2] In terms of worship, the emergent model makes freer use of elements of tradition — possibly ancient, often eclectic. Emergent worship exhibits greater theological flexibility and diversity. It typically makes more room for silence and meditation. And it generally favors a more intimate scale and setting, rather than focusing on large crowds and eye-catching production values.

It should be obvious by now that there is no one "next church" or just one "emergent church" (which is something the "emergent"

2. For more views, both convergent and contrasting, on the Emerging Church and Emergent Christianity, see Dan Kimball, *The Emerging Church: Vintage Christianity for New Generations* (Grand Rapids: Zondervan, 2003); *The Emerging Christian Way*, ed. Michael Schwartzentruber (Kelowna, B.C., Canada: Copperhouse, 2006), with essays by Marcus Borg, Sallie McFague, Matthew Fox, and others; and *The Church in Emerging Culture: Five Perspectives*, ed. Leonard Sweet (Grand Rapids: Zondervan, 2003).

group in particular acknowledges). Ours is a highly fluid and pluralistic time, even though large numbers of Christians identify with one group or another. It seems doubtful that, behind the sometimes monolithic façade created by a given label, there is really a closely unified practice or uniform mind-set among any of these movements.

One other thing that is becoming clear, in any case, is the growing need for more adequate reflection on matters such as artistic media and style (as related to content, not divorced from it), and the aesthetic dimensions of worship and the spiritual life. Such things, which pertain to *how* faith is creatively expressed and enacted, and not only *what* is believed or done, have always been of religious significance. They have nonetheless rarely been a major part of training in Christianity or in theology itself. They don't rank with doctrine and morality on the list of what Christians are taught. And they can seem entirely peripheral, which sometimes they are. But it turns out they matter. And the primary reason they matter is that the very "content" of religious identity and belief is something conveyed and shaped to a significant extent by the *way* it is imagined, narrated, pictured, and sung. What John Witvliet says about the various kinds of music Christians employ could apply to other arts as well — namely, that "they are the pulse of faith, integral to the different ways in which Christians have experienced worship and God's presence for over two thousand years."[3] The form and style of worship and art are not just so many external husks that contain the kernels of the gospel message. On the contrary, they give audible and visible body to the realities and commitments of faith. The very message and person of Christ, along with a Christian sense of life and world, come alive for individuals and communities in image, song, symbol, and story. What Christians classically term the "word of God" thus accommodates itself to many revealing forms, as does the sacramental character of divine presence.

Aesthetics, which is the discipline most attentive to creative and sen-

---

3. John Witvliet, "Beyond Style: Rethinking the Role of Music in Worship," in *Worship at the Next Level: Insight from Contemporary Voices,* ed. Tim A. Dearborn and Scott Coil (Grand Rapids: Baker Books, 2004), pp. 163-79.

sory form in imaginative expression, is therefore of primary significance in acknowledging and interpreting transformative modes of divine self-communication and their gracious and good effects. This is
not to say that theological analysis as such is unimportant; indeed,
such analysis (augmented, perhaps, by interpretation theory or "her-
meneutics") is a necessary part of, and partner in, theological and liturgical aesthetics. But the import of theological ideas registers most
fully as they are envisioned, narrated, and enacted, often in artful media that bring faith to its senses.

What I offer here, therefore, has chiefly to do with the arts, especially as employed in worship. But the ideas I put forward also have indirectly to do with theology and worship in a larger sense, and with
the place of arts and aesthetics (broadly speaking) in the Christian life
as a whole.

In this book I make considerable effort to take into account diverse
perspectives and to build bridges. I like to think my work and training
give me some preparation to do so. For those curious about such
things, it is probably relevant that, as a professor of religion and the
arts in an ecumenical Protestant school of theology affiliated with the
Christian Church (Disciples of Christ), I regularly teach students from
approximately forty different denominations, and across a wide theological and cultural spectrum. Simultaneously, as a visiting professor
of religion and the arts/aesthetics at the University of Chicago Divinity School, which has no church affiliation, I try to be attentive to
how religious and artistic practice is situated in the larger cultural
context. A semester in 2003 as a visiting professor of theology and the
arts at St. John's School of Theology-Seminary enriched my awareness of the Catholic tradition and its arts and worship in ways I have
appreciated ever more fully as time has passed. Finally, my past experience as a choral director and composer-in-residence for several
churches has shaped my sense of the possibilities — and challenges —
of church music.

This book is an outgrowth of a line of thought that began with *Religious Aesthetics: A Theological Study of Making and Meaning* (1989)
and that continued with *Good Taste, Bad Taste, and Christian Taste:*

Aesthetics in Religious Life (2000).[4] The present book is the most practical of the three: the one most attentive to the arts in worship, and to worship that is artful. Even so, it remains concerned with basic principles and with articulating and applying a theological aesthetic that, I hope, will have teeth but no fangs. I offer guidelines and interpretations, and I raise questions, but I believe that specific artistic and liturgical decisions mostly need to be made in view of a particular worshiping community, or at least a particular tradition.

Many of my colleagues at Christian Theological Seminary have commented patiently and insightfully on portions of this book. I want to thank, in particular (and in alphabetical order), Ron Allen, Brian Grant, Holly Hearon, Michael Miller, Dan Moseley, Lorna Shoemaker, and Marti Steussy for dialogue that pushed me to think further and to revise ideas as well as sentences, even if not always in ways they would prefer. Several classes of seminary students have likewise given me an invaluable mix of appreciative and questioning feedback. Elsewhere, seasoned scholars and practitioners of arts and worship such as Jeremy Begbie, Melva Costin, Charlotte Kroeker, Anthony Ruff, Don Saliers, Kevin Seasoltz, Janet Walton, and Paul Westermeyer have helped me more than they know both with their words and by their example. Eleonore Stump has prodded me, philosophically, to ponder further the mysterious powers of music to animate — or sometimes to deflate — the spirit. I am especially grateful to John Witvliet, who is with the Calvin Institute for Worship and is editor of the Institute's Liturgical Studies series for Eerdmans. His support and encouragement have been crucial.

Much of what follows originated in guest lectures, whose sponsoring organizations I need and want to acknowledge. These lectures include plenary addresses at the annual meeting of the North American Academy of Liturgy; at the annual, international meeting of the Hymn Societies of the USA and Canada, Great Britain, and Ireland; at an in-

---

4. Frank Burch Brown, *Religious Aesthetics: A Theological Study of Making and Meaning* (Princeton, N.J.: Princeton University Press, 1989); Brown, *Good Taste, Bad Taste, and Christian Taste*.

ternational conference on theological aesthetics in Denver, Colorado; at the annual Calvin Symposium on Worship in Grand Rapids, Michigan; and at a symposium called "Singing God's Song Faithfully" sponsored by the Institute for Church Life at the University of Notre Dame. There were also established lectureships where I tried out ideas that reappear here: the Royal Humbert Lecture at Eureka College; the Norman Mealey Lecture at St. Mark's Episcopal Church, Berkeley; and the Woods Lectures at the University of Dubuque Theological Seminary, Iowa. Other material derives from invited lectures at the Yale Institute of Sacred Music; at the Sacred Music Institute of the University of Iowa; at Union Theological Seminary, Richmond, Virginia; at St. John's Abbey (the Benedictine monastery at St. John's University, Collegeville, Minnesota); and at an *Imago Dei* conference at the St. Paul School of Theology, Kansas City, Missouri. I thank these organizations, many of which were equipped for multimedia presentations that, regrettably, cannot fully be translated into text form.

Earlier versions of various chapters in this book first appeared elsewhere. I thank the editors and publishers who have granted me permission to reprint them, revised.

Finally, a word about the dedication. Everyone in my family of origin had a love of music, which my brother and I frequently demonstrated by discussing (and, to my mother's dismay, arguing about) musical works and performances with an intensity that might surprise others. But my mother, to whose memory this book is dedicated, was the one who had the clearest commitment to church music. She also had a keen sense that what we do with music in worship, and how we do it, can matter very much — not only to ourselves, but in some sense even to God, or possibly to God most of all.

Inclusive yet Discerning

Albrecht Dürer, *Self-Portrait* **(as Christ), 1500, oil on panel,**
Alte Pinakothek, Munich (photo courtesy of Artothek)

In making a kind of icon of himself as artist bearing the image of Christ,
Dürer asks us, in effect, to discern whether his beautiful painting is an act
of devotion — of aspiring to be Christ-like — or a display of his technical
skill as an internationally famous artist at age 28, or somehow both.

CHAPTER I

Navigating Worship Artfully:
Finding a Compass

A Sea of Options and the Need for a Compass

One of the remarkable features of our time is the widespread and often easy access to a vast and variegated array of arts and styles that are intended to enliven and nourish the spirit. In the sphere of music alone, one can hear everything from ancient "Old Roman" chant and Peruvian church music composed in a baroque style by indigenous Indians to contemporary Christian grunge rock and Palestinian social protest rap, not to mention masses in polka or flamenco style and the latest "Indipop" spiritual songs from South Asia (perhaps using electronic synthesizers and blending with New Age meditative styles). There is no doubt that more arts and media are accessible to more people now than ever before, from across the world and from almost every known period of history. This is due in no small part to the ongoing revolution in digital reproduction, electronic communication, and Internet distribution, as well as to the "shrinking" of the globe through travel, trade, migration, and networks of economic and environmental interdependence across the world.

As religious groups encounter increasingly diverse options, often in the midst of truly multicultural communities, they naturally consider whether and how to become more diverse themselves, and not least in the arts employed in worship. This is not only for the sake of attracting more youth or of enhancing worship through artistic variety; it is also out of a desire to include a broader social spectrum in worship — at least as broad as their surrounding communities — and to grow spiritually and liturgically in ways in which the arts are uniquely gifted. Traditions otherwise resistant to change can thus be found experimenting. One can witness very traditional Presbyterians move to incorporate Taizé musical refrains from France and can be astonished to encounter Eastern Orthodox attempts at Christian rock. Even groups already identified with change may change further in surprising ways, as in Reform Jewish excursions into Broadway-style musical idioms.

However worthwhile, such attempts at broader inclusion and artistic exploration are fraught with risks.[1] While the first word in introducing a wider range of artistic expression, in many contexts, needs to be a word of welcome for the art in question, the welcome often needs to be conditional — which by no means precludes "unconditional love" for those involved. Each different mode of art and music requires, inevitably, a certain sort of attunement that needs to be learned through practice, accompanied by a measure of goodwill. Even in a congregation familiar with hip-hop culture, for example, rap that is introduced in the context of worship is unlikely to find itself immediately at home, or to fulfill whatever potential it may have for "edgy" protest or social critique, without a degree of congregational preparation and conditioning. A different kind of preparation might be called for in certain congregations prior to a choir's singing a Latin *Gloria* by Vivaldi, which in some contexts might otherwise tend to be received as a relic from a bygone era or a mere performance.

In view of the risks and almost inevitable tensions, why not simply maintain the status quo, or settle once and for all on a small repertoire of suitably representative styles? At the very least, why not wait for a definitive body of informed ecclesial opinion to point the way? These

---

1. For descriptions and, at points, critiques of such musical innovations in the recent past, see *Sacred Sound and Social Change: Liturgical Music in Jewish and Christian Experience*, ed. Lawrence A. Hoffman and Janet R. Walton (Notre Dame, Ind.: University of Notre Dame Press, 1992).

questions are not unreasonable. Historically, the dominant churches and indeed whole religions have been able to expect worshipers, however different, to submit their personal preferences and sensibilities to a common style or repertoire widely recognized by religious leaders as fitting for that tradition and place, or sacred in character. To a remarkable extent, that relative uniformity of worship practice still characterizes Islam today, despite various differences between Sunni and Shiite Muslims.

Yet the present situation is in some ways genuinely new. For one thing, the arts in the modern era have flourished so extensively in secular settings that fewer people are prepared to accept without question the aesthetic judgments of their religious leaders and professional church musicians, particularly when they rule out styles that are deemed too "worldly." And in truth, religious leaders may be relatively inexperienced and uninformed when it comes to the arts. At the same time, professional musicians and artists cannot be expected to be competent in all styles or to have a comprehensive theological education. More than ever, they need to consult with others on matters of both art and liturgy.

New developments are likewise relevant to the issue of when to seek arts with wider appeal in worship, and whether that entails diversifying a church's repertoire. Uniformity and restraint may be a good, "inclusive" option in the most conservative of traditional religious groups, such as Russian Orthodox. At least in much of the West, however, music and other arts in our time have been segmented as never before into countless niche markets associated with specific age and ethnic groups, or with particular cultural and social identities. The cross-cultural and cross-generational blockbuster such as Mel Gibson's 2004 film *Passion of the Christ* and the current Harry Potter phenomenon (whether the books or the films) may be the dream of many a film studio or publisher — whatever worries it may cause certain Christians. But promoters of the arts are increasingly (if somewhat precariously) reliant on intense niche marketing, as the multiplication of subgenres within popular music attests. In the words of David Shumway, "The cultural position of popular music and its stars has diminished. . . . What we have long considered to be mass culture has increasingly become a collection of niche cultures." Shumway goes on to declare, "One could argue that the term 'popular music' itself has become outdated because no style of music reaches a broad enough audience."[2] Each listener today can compile his or her own immediately accessible "playlist" of favorites on CD or iPod, for instance, which is tailored to that person's tastes alone, thereby privatizing the act of listening to an unprecedented extent — instead of depending on a communally shared experience or corporate set of expectations, which even radio had tended to create.

This situation in music, which is replicated to a certain extent in other arts, affects churches, since market segmentation and the privatization of taste militate against shared and communally practiced arts and styles. Considering the extent of niche marketing in the secular world, it is no wonder that church members and subgroups within congregations typically bring with them a desire to have their own musical tastes and art preferences represented in worship. By the same token, however, it is equally clear why churches cannot simply assume that any particular musical style or blend of idioms will easily or automatically attain cross-cultural and intergenerational acceptance in worship.

There is another aspect of the secular market in music and art that has a bearing on worship. According to Shumway, the most interesting and culturally significant art and music today — even for people without special training — is rarely the kind that is most popular in terms of cultural visibility (or audibility). In popular music, "those whose recordings now top the charts usually seem to be the least culturally significant, often lacking either the musical distinction or the political commentary that one can still find among less popular performers."[3] For churches taking their cue from music marketing as they reach out to attract large congregations, the situation in the music industry

2. David Shumway, "Where Have All the Rock Stars Gone?" *Chronicle of Higher Education*, June 22, 2007 (http://chronicle.com/weekly/v53/i42/42b00601.htm).
3. Shumway, "Where Have All the Rock Stars Gone?"

could be sobering. Lynn Hirschberg reports that, as of 2007, "the mighty music business is in free fall — it has lost control of radio; retail outlets like Tower Records have shut down; MTV rarely broadcasts music videos; and the once lucrative album market has been overshadowed by downloaded singles, which mainly benefits Apple." Hirschberg then quotes the legendary music mogul David Geffen as stating, "Panic has set in, and now it's no longer about making music, it's all about how to sell music. And there's no clear answer about how to fix that problem."[4] It is understandable that churches have been tempted to do what the advertising and entertainment industries have done: employ music that features catchy "hooks" but aspires to little artistically, and that in substance is reduced to something like the lowest common denominator. But while many churches have made that kind of compromise in order to attract crowds, evidence is mounting that, as Shumway argues, the music with widest popular appeal today is often the least substantial and the least creative. And that is a significant price to pay, in worship, if one believes that the quality of the medium affects the quality of the message.

We can now see more clearly why, when it comes to seeking a more inclusive practice of worship arts, the need to reach out must be held in creative tension with an accompanying need to become more discerning and — in the best sense — discriminating in selecting and cultivating the arts for worship. This does not mean insisting that every art offered in church display a high degree of polish and skill. The question of discernment in worship is not only about intrinsic artistic quality but also about appropriateness. Arts such as dance and video, when newly introduced in church, will seldom display the same level of skill or accomplishment that arts such as choral singing do — arts that have long played an integral part in worship. Yet the arts that represent newer ventures may be highly appropriate in principle, and worthwhile in spite of the challenges. It takes time for congregations and artists alike to learn how a given art can be shaped to the highest

---

4. Lynn Hirschberg, "The Music Man: Can Rick Rubin Save the Record Business?" *New York Times Magazine,* September 2, 2007, p. 28.

purposes of worship and practiced at a level that can begin to do justice to the art itself, as a worship medium.

Discernment is called for not only because a given form of art may need to grow into its full potential for worship but also because, as we have already observed, not all that glitters will ever be gold, artistically speaking. There is no use denying that much of the art and music appearing in churches around the world today reproduces artistic styles that, in the long run, have relatively little to commend them in the context of worship. At a popular level, secular styles are too often adopted uncritically, simply because they have captivated some group's attention and are appealing in some way. At the same time, much of the most prevalent "high art" of our day is esoteric, difficult, and demanding, and in its own way faddish. Meanwhile, the more conventional kinds of church artistry come across to many worshipers as bland, boring, and unadventurous. It is not always easy to tell which arts and styles hold genuine promise, and which need to be excused early, or perhaps retired after years or indeed centuries of valuable service.

What makes discernment even more difficult is precisely the sometimes hard-won awareness that good art, including art good for worship, can take many forms, not all of which co-exist peacefully in the same space or time. There are various appropriate classic and contemporary patterns of music, but these do not all converge or harmonize. Gregorian chant and contemporary gospel do not readily "blend." Singing any form of chant in a service, moreover, requires adequate time and often calls for an ambience of silence. Similarly, one cannot, in the interest of time, adopt a speeded-up service of praise and worship choruses (eliminating all the repetitions, for instance) and still preserve the essential contour and flow.

Equally complicating, when it comes to establishing norms, is the fact that, try as we might, we cannot actually replicate some "original" pattern or template of art or worship that derives from Scripture and that could plausibly be held to be timeless, or even truly ancient. The Psalms survive mainly as words, with only hints of how the voices and instruments were employed. Jesus left only brief instructions on how to pray, and none at all on how to sing. No one quite knows what

8

New Testament music sounded like, or many details regarding how early Christians worshiped. Even if a trove of scores of the earliest Christian music were discovered, decoded, and interpreted success-fully in our time — perhaps as a musical counterpart to the Dead Sea Scrolls — no one could recreate how that song actually sounded to congregations of an earlier era and geographical setting.[5] The art of the past is necessarily heard and experienced differently when recre-ated in the present, accustomed as we now are to a constant bombard-ment of media messages.

Finally, to make matters even more challenging, the standards for artistic excellence can never fully be put into words. As philosophers since Immanuel Kant have realized, there are no exhaustive or invari-able rules determinative of beauty or artistic excellence. And aesthetic judgments need to be so finely tuned to the specifics of the aesthetic medium that there is no hope of spelling out their basis completely in the medium of words and abstract concepts. The same holds true for the "rules" devised for church arts specifically.

Contrary to what is often assumed, however, the major problem in distinguishing good art from bad is not that the arts are so subjective or that aesthetic judgments are entirely relative and beyond meaning-ful discussion or dispute. After all, no one knows exactly how anyone else subjectively experiences true love or the act of genuine forgive-ness, yet the quality and reality of those things, while without objec-tive measure, are immeasurably important and rightly the subject of much human conversation and attention.

Fortunately, aesthetic values and judgments can be tested inter-subjectively (something Kant would affirm regarding judgments of beauty in general). And they may, in their own way, point to some-

5. There have been speculative but aesthetically rewarding attempts at reconstruct-ing music for psalms and other texts from the Hebrew Bible (Old Testament), as well as from the time of Jesus. Of special interest are two recordings: *The Music of the Bible: A Thousand-Year-old Notation Deciphered by Suzanne Haïk Vantoura*, Harmonia Mundi France, HMA 195989 (1976); and Savae (San Antonio Vocal Arts Ensemble), *Ancient Echoes: Music from the Time of Jesus and Jerusalem's Second Temple*, World Library Publications, WLP 002348 (2002).

thing beyond sheer subjectivity. I happen to hold that the Southern spiritual song "Wayfaring Stranger," as I heard my mother sing it at home — and my uncle, once, in church — is really poignant, haunting, and beautiful. It is a song whose beauty (whatever "beauty" means) I would hope God recognizes and affirms in some sense, even though it would play a different role in the divine life than in ours. But even if, after all, there weren't any humanly created beauty that God could be thought to affirm and enjoy as such, it would still be true that human beings often tend to register the qualities in music and other arts in similar ways, despite personal and cultural variations. If that were not the case, movie music, for instance, would be completely useless or distracting. There would be no predicting how people would respond to a particular passage of music. Neither the composer of the sound-track nor the movie director could ever anticipate whether the particular music that rises in intensity as Batman comes to the rescue or as Lassie at last finds her way home would actually reinforce the sense of emotional relief and exhilaration, or would instead seem incongruous. The relative effectiveness of most soundtracks is ample testimony to a rather widely shared range of aesthetic "tastes" among human beings, by and large.

What is misleading about this is that it does not translate into in-variable rules. Indeed, few informed worship leaders today believe that various older prescriptions and prohibitions for sacred art are, strictly speaking, universal, as was formerly supposed — the once-common idea, for instance, that only music explicitly composed for sacred purposes has a legitimate role in church, or that pianos (or woodwinds) are inherently secular, or that gentle, quiet music is almost always the most reverent and worshipful.

But if the Bible itself is vague about how worship and its arts are to be carried out, and if enduring norms and rules seem hard to come by, how is one to find guidance in responding to the call to glorify God artistically in worship? One thing we can reasonably hope for, at present, is to come up with a kind of compass for navigating worship artfully: guidelines that point us in promising directions and that we have reason to believe are in touch with underlying principles that are relatively secure. And even then, since errors and misjudgments are inevitable, a degree of humility and a sense of humor will be indispensable.

Perhaps the kind of compass most useful at this stage of the discussion would be a guide identifying attitudes toward the arts and worship that are predictably ineffective or harmful, and those that are almost invariably effective or helpful from the standpoint of both religion and aesthetics. Accordingly, I want in the remainder of this chapter to revisit and expand on a topic I addressed almost two decades ago, in my book *Religious Aesthetics,* in a chapter entitled "Sin and Bad Taste."[6] With the advantage of hindsight, I now want to fill out the positive side, instead of dwelling only on the problems. I proceed with a nod (in terminology only) to the popular book *Seven Habits of Highly Effective People* by Stephen Covey, and with another, respectful nod to the incomparably more substantial *Divine Comedy* by Dante, whose account of the nature and consequences of certain vices and virtues is memorable indeed. Accordingly, I will discuss, on the one hand, a set of four ineffective habits in approaching art and worship (habits that in traditional terminology could be called vices), and then will identify, on the other hand, the corresponding effective habits (which in traditional terminology could be termed virtues). I have every confidence that Dante, while reflecting a distinctive medieval perspective, would agree with my assumption here that the arts matter more to the quality and character of worship than is widely recognized, and that there are vices and virtues associated with different approaches to any art that matters. Unlike Dante, however, I will not propose particular rewards or punishments but will concentrate on acknowledging the potential joy and transformative role of worship itself, and the disappointment (and possible harm done) when that potential is not fulfilled.

---

6. Frank Burch Brown, *Religious Aesthetics: A Theological Study of Making and Meaning* (Princeton, N.J.: Princeton University Press, 1989), pp. 136-57.

Empty Aestheticism versus Authentic Aesthetic Spirituality

The first habit I would identify as ineffective and unproductive, and frankly harmful, is the vice exemplified by the aesthete. This is the person whose chief goal in approaching art in worship is not glorifying and enjoying God, but glorying in the beauties of art to the exclusion of all else, including morality and religion. Aestheticism is different from seeing a given work of beautiful or expressive art as in some ways valuable in itself and thus as having a God-given right to exist, without always needing an ulterior purpose. Rather, aestheticism in the sense intended here is a refusal to perceive or savor anything about art (even art used in worship) other than strictly its own beautiful or expressive form or the play of aesthetic imagination.

The aesthete's habit of mind worried the nineteenth-century Christian philosopher Søren Kierkegaard a great deal. As we will note again in a later chapter, Kierkegaard, living in an era in which the most celebrated artists had frequently come to be seen as geniuses or even prophets in their own right, knew that an appreciation of art could terminate just there, and so stop short of a higher religious purpose. He considered that an artist painting a portrait of Christ might focus exclusively on the artistry itself.[7] The artist might pay more attention to matters of color and composition, or plausible human likeness, than to conveying any purpose Christ had in either living or dying. We might consider, for instance, Albrecht Dürer's famous if enigmatic self-portrait of himself as Christ (reproduced at the beginning of this chapter). Art connoisseurs admiring the oil painting could be impressed with the expression on the face or the immaculate and scarcely visible brushwork that went into depicting the elegant locks of hair and the fur collar. They might be so taken by the artistry that they would not give the slightest thought to envisioning the person of Christ or perceiving someone as truly remade in the image of Christ. Granted, no one knows the occasion or intended setting for this partic-

---

7. Søren Kierkegaard, *Practice in Christianity*, ed. and trans. Howard V. Hong and Edna H. Hong (Princeton, N.J.: Princeton University Press, 1991), p. 255.

ular painting, which Kierkegaard did not discuss. But even when viewing such a work in the context of a worship space, its combination of utter artistic mastery with its frontal presentation of a beautiful and seemingly self-possessed human countenance might allure one into relishing such artistry in oblivion of all else, without attending to any religious meaning it might have — perhaps as a creative and provocative variant on the venerable ideal of the "imitation of Christ."[8]

The problem of aestheticism is exacerbated by the formerly pervasive modernist idea that a genuine appreciation of art as such will treat all other factors as extraneous, such as whether it is meant to encourage adoration or positive "imitation" of Christ. In any case, the aesthetic enjoyment of art to the exclusion of religion is by no means confined to the visual arts. Many clergy and worship leaders, for example, have commented with good reason on the potentially distracting effects of elaborate or ostentatious church music on the mental state of congregants ostensibly in the act of worship. In Leipzig in the time of J. S. Bach, some Lutheran clergy became worried that more people were coming to church to hear the cantata on Sunday than to hear the sermon. (That might not have been altogether a bad thing, if they were listening with "spiritual" ears; but that is precisely the question.) In our day, several well-known organists have made public statements to the effect that music is their religion. And a fair number of choral directors at festivals and even in churches seem indifferent to whether the choir actually conveys the inner meaning of the music it sings, whether that be Handel's *Messiah* or the latest gospel favorite. A similar concern arises on those occasions when praise bands are evidently transported by nothing so much as the sheer excitement of the sound they're producing and by virtuosic vocal displays. Whenever worship music becomes merely performance, that is a form of aestheticism.

There is a positive counterpart to the vice of the aesthete, however. That is the "effective habit" or virtue found in the person who has a

---

8. For a fascinating and detailed study of this work and its intriguing ambiguities, see Joseph Leo Koerner, *The Moment of Self-Portraiture in German Renaissance Art* (Chicago: University of Chicago Press, 1993), pp. 63-79.

genuinely aesthetic spirituality. This is the approach of a person or group whose devotion is expressed artistically, among other things, and who discovers in music and art, and possibly in beautiful nature as well, a medium by which to glorify God and to commune with others.

A Sacred Harp singing convention that the ethnomusicologist Alan Lomax recorded in rural northern Alabama back in 1959 provides a good example of this way of practicing music worshipfully. In the recording, as edited by Lomax, we first hear the testimony of a local woman who expresses gratitude that singing can sometimes take hold when a sermon might just pass a person right on by. She has been sick a long time, and she thanks her community for trying to teach her to sing, and for standing by her in prayer. Then everyone breaks out singing the song "Wondrous Love," with words from the mid-nineteenth century and a tune from still longer ago. Their voices join together, even if they do not blend: "What wondrous love is this, O my soul, O my soul,/What wondrous love is this, O my soul?/What wondrous love is this that caused the Lord of bliss/To lay aside his life for my soul, for my soul,/To lay aside his life for my soul?" These singers have gone to country singing school; they have also trained each other. It makes a difference. But this is shaped-note singing (given that name because of how it is notated on the page), and its sound is astringent, not refined. Indeed, it strikes the ear as fiery, fierce, and untamed.[9] It is certainly not beautiful in the usual sense of smooth or harmonious or splendidly refined. It is beautiful through a raw intensity that, in effect, burns away cheap sentiment and that suggests, by its very tone and character, a reliance on God and on the community for endurance. The result is musical devotion in which the artistry makes no apology for itself but gives itself over to something larger than art alone, which makes singing of this kind possible to begin with.

9. *White Spirituals from Sacred Harp*, recorded and annotated by Alan Lomax, 1959. Reissued by New World Records, 1977; see CD booklet, pp. 2-3.

Philistine Disdain versus Devotion to and through Art

The second ineffective habit or vice in matters of art and worship is that of the philistine — to use the customary terminology (originally from the biblical term *Philistine,* not in reference to the Palestinian peoples of modern times). If the aesthete comes to worship only for the art, and worships beauty without any sense of its divine source and goal, the philistine commonly treats any regard for art and beauty as worthless in comparison with a firm system of beliefs, acts of righteousness, and a will to conduct oneself morally. In worship, the philistine regards art as little more than a low-level aid to worship, however pleasant, and listens for God's true "word" not in the hymns or anthems but only when the sermon is preached.

In the film *Babette's Feast* (Gabriel Axel, 1987), which I have elsewhere discussed from a different perspective[10] and which has caught the attention of Christian film critics from the time of its initial release, we see a strongly ascetic bent to life and worship among a tenacious little religious community in Jutland, Denmark, to which the French chef Babette comes after fleeing from political chaos in France. Those devoted people, very disciplined in prayer and works of charity, are nonetheless portrayed as the epitome of what we can call a philistine sensibility. They deny themselves the pleasures of the senses in favor of another world and a God high and lifted up. Even more, they reject amorous love and the kinds of songs conducive to that — exemplified by seductive songs from Mozart's *Don Giovanni.* Instead, they dutifully commit themselves to a rigorous life together that eventually wears the spirit thin and that breeds dissention. Babette, after learning she has won a lottery she had long forgotten about, is inspired to whet the spiritual and physical senses of the community by producing a feast that becomes at once a work of "art" and, in effect, a quasi-sacrament. The transformation wrought by the feast reveals that the community, in its denial of the senses, had also sacrificed something vi-

---

10. Frank Burch Brown, *Good Taste, Bad Taste, and Christian Taste: Aesthetics in Religious Life* (New York: Oxford University Press, 2000), pp. 265-70.

tal to the fulfillment of life and of worship itself — a spirit-filled pleasure, eros, and beauty that in a strictly practical sense can seem excessive and superfluous. And yet what the artful feast provides the spirit
is more than sensuality in the worldly sense, which lacks the depth and
purpose of the realm of faith.

The alternative to the philistine is the person who, far from disdain-
ing art, is intensely devoted to according art and beauty their own
rightful place, even when they appear completely useless. In Alice
Walker's novel *The Color Purple,* which has long been regarded as a
significant landmark of modern literature, there is a famous passage in
which the character Shug says — and here I'm retaining Walker's
rather salty but vivid language — "I think it pisses God off if you walk
by the color purple in a field somewhere and don't notice it."[11] The act
of noticing beauty, and letting gratitude and praise flow from that, is
what allows even simple Shaker furniture and the clean lines and white
exteriors of classic Calvinist churches to honor God. This is part of
what the Christian (and Calvinist) philosopher Nicholas Wolterstorff
means when he claims that aesthetic delight is part of the peaceful
earthly flourishing or *shalom* that is divinely ordained for human
life.[12] To enjoy beauty, and thereby to enjoy God and God's creation, is
both a duty and a delight.

Aesthetic Intolerance versus Hospitality

A third kind of harmful, ineffective habit that begs for attention is exemplified by those who are intolerant. The intolerant person, who typically seeks out others who are intolerant in the same way, may be
someone who is keenly aware of aesthetic standards and wants only
the best art in worship. Earlier in American and European history, the
highest — or at least most conspicuous — level of aesthetic intolerance

11. Alice Walker, *The Color Purple,* reprint ed. (New York: Washington Square
Press/Pocket Books, 1983), p. 178.
12. Nicholas Wolterstorff, *Art in Action: Toward a Christian Aesthetic* (Grand
Rapids: William B. Eerdmans, 1980), p. 169; cf. pp. 78-83.

was shown by elitist supporters of "high art" such as classical music. In the United States, the latter was often the only music taught in the proliferation of music appreciation classes in colleges in the mid-twentieth century, and was touted by classical radio stations as the only genuinely "good music." However, what stuck was not so much the identification of classical with "good" as an elitism that regarded all alternatives to classical music as bad and that often implied that "classical" meant high class. That was despite the fact that a high percentage of classical musicians and composers since the eighteenth century, while often benefiting from upper-class patronage, have come from middle-class or working-class families and have intended their music to be open to the enjoyment of human beings everywhere. Many classical composers and performers would almost surely support a kind of "Robin Hood" principle by which the best thing would be to make their music widely available to people who in a former time would have lacked the means. And with modern technology, that has become a real possibility, at least in principle, since anyone with access to a CD player or an iPod can listen to top-notch performances of literally thousands of works and performances that formerly only people of means could afford.

One obstacle to turning that potential into reality on a wider basis was the intolerance, historically, of those who had adopted classical music mainly as an accessory, as a sign of prestige and privilege, in the process of rising to middle- or upper-class status. From the mid-nineteenth century through the mid-twentieth century, a large number of Americans and others working their way up the social ladder acquired European-based "high culture" as a means of cultural and social advancement. Classical music, among other things, became an emblem of success, often little appreciated in its own terms as music by the very donors and financial underwriters who made much of it possible.[13] Meanwhile, those people who acquired a taste for the high arts

---

13. The ways in which the "classical" and "elite" arts have been exploited for purposes of class and prestige are documented — albeit in a way that fails to do justice to the intrinsic worth of much of this artistry — in two books in particular: Lawrence W. Levine, *Highbrow/Lowbrow: The Emergence of Cultural Hierarchy in America* (Cam-

through education and practice relished and projected a sense of superiority. Like other aesthetically intolerant people, of whom many composers and architects are notorious examples, they exhibited little interest in acknowledging the extent to which artistic excellence can appear in multiple styles and guises.

Intolerance is not confined to the artistic elite, however. Someone who is intolerant may, in fact, simply be yielding to the common human tendency to like and embrace what we already know, and to scorn or dismiss what is different and unfamiliar. When people say they know what they like in terms of the arts and worship, they are more often than not unconsciously saying they like what they know. And, given the challenges facing an increasingly underfunded curriculum in the arts in education in the United States and elsewhere, an ever-growing number of people these days are entering adulthood knowing less and less about the arts, whether through personal practice or academic study.

The link between everyday inexperience and unexamined intolerance can be seen, again, in the reception of classical music in recent times. Classical music was not generally on the map of "cool stuff" during the formative years of the so-called baby-boomer generation, which developed a strong identity with folk and rock. And its presence in education was spotty at best. As a consequence, it is scarcely understood today in anything like its full range and depth by those same people, who frequently occupy top positions in leading churches, schools, arts organizations, and other cultural institutions. The classics, especially in music, are widely avoided for a stodginess that they have come to symbolize in the popular mind but that has little to do in reality with the long-term vitality of those arts themselves.[14]

---

bridge, Mass.: Harvard University Press, 1988); and Pierre Bourdieu, *Distinction: A Social Critique of the Judgment of Taste,* trans. Richard Nice (Cambridge, Mass.: Harvard University Press, 1984).

14. The institutions of high art and their counterparts in prestigious churches and academic institutions are themselves partly responsible for this. For much of the twentieth century, practitioners of the "high arts" and the institutions supporting them, going back to figures such as Picasso and Stravinsky early in that century, were preoccupied

Some time ago, theologians and other interpreters of culture such as Tex Sample and Robert Walser wrote a spate of books making a case for paying attention to music such as country western and heavy metal, which had largely been marginalized in "respectable" Christian practice and in discussions of music and religion.[15] While that move was legitimate and important, today the situation is reversed, at least with regard to the way classical traditions are now frequently treated. One regularly hears conference speakers hastily dismiss the bulk of classical church music with misleading labels such as "performance music," or with the sweeping judgment that such music is by its nature "culturally irrelevant." The fruits of such intolerance are readily seen, not least in the music featured in many of the new community churches and suburban megachurches. That music typically ignores classical traditions, except possibly when "jazzed up." Casual in character, it is limited to the predictable comfort zone of most suburban, white Americans (even when such churches are racially mixed).

One would never guess from all this that in many parts of Asia, including Japan and China, classical music of Occidental derivation is a huge growth industry. Meanwhile, the irony is that composers and arrangers for movie, television, and video soundtracks still continue to use a large amount of music that is classical in all but name, and much of it new. That is because of the music's wide expressive range and ca-

---

with difficult, avant-garde styles. However rewarding to the initiated, such styles were typically so forbidding that they alienated even much of the educated public, who began to dread "contemporary" art in its high cultural or classical guise and who increasingly turned to vernacular idioms for their own self-expression.

Many writers and scholars deeply familiar with classical music have begun to make efforts to counteract the unduly negative and distorted image it has acquired. See Lawrence Kramer, *Why Classical Music Still Matters* (Berkeley and Los Angeles: University of California Press, 2007); Joshua Fineberg, *Classical Music, Why Bother?* (New York: Routledge, 2006); and Melanie Lowe, *Pleasure and Meaning in the Classical Symphony* (Bloomington: Indiana University Press, 2007).

15. See, for instance, Tex Sample, *White Soul: Country Music, the Church, and Working Americans* (Nashville, Tenn.: Abingdon Press, 1996); and Robert Walser, *Running with the Devil: Power, Gender, and Madness in Heavy Metal Music* (Hanover, N.H.: Wesleyan University Press/University Press of New England, 1993).

pacity to convey emotions, whether subtle or sweeping. And this is true, remarkably, at the most popular level. So it is that Howard Shore's music for the trilogy *Lord of the Rings* (Peter Jackson, 2003-2006) and Hans Zimmer's soundtrack for the latest installment of *Pirates of the Caribbean* (*At World's End*, Disney Productions, 2007), not to mention the large number of soundtracks by John Williams for such favorites as the multi-part *Star Wars* series, all include music in broadly classical idioms (as well as folk, fusion, and ethnically influenced styles). A good argument could be made, moreover, that this music for public entertainment is at times more moving and serious than much of what one hears in churches today. Such music, because it bypasses the label "classical," circumvents the intolerance of what people imagine "classical" music to be like.

The virtue that is a counterpart and an answer to intolerance is artistic and aesthetic hospitality. Hospitality does not mean accepting every kind of music and art that others like, without question or criticism. Instead, as an extension of the will and habit of love, it means learning more about what others care for, and finding a middle ground where, with patience and practice, we can transcend initial reactions of distaste or even revulsion. In that way we can gradually learn to discern, without necessarily liking it ourselves, what others appreciate about a given kind of art or music.

It is worth considering in this connection that the process of responding to a work of art (whether in worship or not) entails three elements, which I have identified — using alliteration — as apperception, appreciation, and appraisal.[16] In apperception, we take in everything relevant to whatever makes the work of art the thing it is — the work itself. In appreciation, we register our personal likes or dislikes of the work. Those may be quite variable and eccentric. In appraisal, we render a judgment as to the work's merits, or lack thereof, in a manner meant to have public validity and to transcend our personal eccentricities. Hospitality involves all three aspects of "taste" in this sense. To cultivate greater hospitality, one must learn to perceive more of what

16. See Brown, *Good Taste, Bad Taste, and Christian Taste*, pp. 12-24.

the work has to offer, as guided by the responses and judgments of those most familiar with the idiom. And one must learn the ability to set aside personal likes as necessary, since those are highly subject to whim and bias. Finally, one must learn to postpone a considered appraisal until one gains sufficient experience — or perhaps realizes that, with respect to a particularly unfamiliar style or form of art, one may never be in a position to make a sound appraisal. All of these acts conducive to aesthetic hospitality can be cultivated in church communities, ideally under shared leadership.

We should have no illusions about this. We are not put together in such a way as to like or even tolerate everything others like. Tastes in music and art — especially in worship music — reflect and create genuine differences, culturally reinforced. They help shape our sense of corporate and religious identity. Yet going beyond initial reactions can bring about growth in that it can lead to a gradual expansion of one's own horizons on art and worship. And learning to accept — and even relish — differences in terms of the arts in worship is essential to any church community that aspires to show in its corporate and artistic life a high degree of hospitality toward diversity.

Indiscriminate Taste versus Caring Discernment

We have examined the harmful and ineffective habit of aestheticism and contrasted that with the virtue of an aesthetic spirituality. We have discussed the philistine's attitude and countered that vice with the virtue of an ardent and devoted appreciation of beauty and art. We next drew attention to the ineffective habit or vice of intolerance as that shows up in art and worship, and contrasted that with aesthetic and religious hospitality: a willingness to extend respect and to welcome more of the arts and practices of others by cultivating skills of apperception, appreciation, and appraisal.

My final example of an ineffective habit is the opposite of intolerance. It is the fault we can identify as being indiscriminate. This is the harmful habit or vice that in many settings is the greatest temptation for Christians today. That is because it seems so loving. It looks deceptively virtuous. It can easily seem that the good Christian should surrender artistic priorities in an act of charity and so accept whatever artistry people care to offer God in worship, regardless of source or style. In later chapters, especially in examining whether good art is good for Christian worship, I will examine a number of different versions of this Christian temptation. For now I will try to explain briefly why it is so alluring to many Christians and yet is by no means innocuous.

The temptation to be indiscriminate in the arts of worship is powerful because it can be supported by seemingly good religious reasons. First, the question of artistic quality and appropriateness can seem of minor significance compared with much else in worship and the Christian life. The Bible offers practically no guidelines in this area. Jesus seems to assume that his disciples can sing, but he never instructs them on repertoire or cautions them about poor intonation or warns against using their voices and gestures in an overly worldly or superficially entertaining way.

Second, while Christians have fought bitterly over which arts to allow in worship, the worship wars have often seemed petty and symptomatic of unseemly power plays rather than a manifestation of genuine piety. To rectify that, and in the interests of peacemaking, it often just seems easier and more virtuous in the long run to surrender than to fight (as if those were the only two alternatives).

Third, as we have already noted, the very grounds for distinguishing good arts from bad are hard to discern reliably. There are many factors to consider, including cultural context. And the specifically artistic reasons for making choices are not the ones most easily identified and explained, theologically and liturgically. One can compose a communion song that is theologically sound in its text, easily sung and remembered, suitably short (or long), and so forth — and yet the song might still be little more than a string of musical and devotional clichés. It can be hard to explain why this artistic inferiority can matter, religiously. Yet almost everyone intuitively knows, on the basis of perhaps limited experience, that the quality of a communion song can make all the difference between a moment that is merely functional, liturgically speaking, and a moment in which the very meaning of the act of communion is expressed and conveyed in the song itself. It is the slippery nature of that kind of aesthetic judgment that encourages an uncritical and indiscriminate practice on the part of worship leaders. They may prefer to sidestep aesthetic issues to avoid misunderstanding or conflict (which at times is undoubtedly the right choice).

A fourth factor that lends itself to indiscriminate artistic practice surfaces in the following question: Doesn't the idea that the gospel is for everyone mean that everything in a worship service must likewise be for everyone? Without getting into the specifics of this vexed question, which comes back in various guises throughout this book, I simply want to observe here that, as in everything, there are extremes that we should take care to avoid. Worship should rarely feature an artistic elite presenting something that is meaningful only to a small inner circle, or give preference to the few doing even what the many could easily do themselves. But neither should the art and music of worship always be limited to what the average person can do and instantly appreciate. As we will later see in exploring the views of Pope Benedict XVI on art and worship, such a stipulation would tend to promote mediocrity and would unduly restrict the aesthetic dimensions of corporate worship, as well as curtailing the possibilities of Christian growth in and through the arts.

I have recommended alternatives and antidotes to all the other ineffective habits or vices: those of the aesthete, the philistine, and the intolerant. What then is the antidote to being indiscriminate, and thus to accepting practically every work or style of art in worship, at least when it is offered with a good heart and is somehow likeable? The alternative should be obvious by now. It is to be discerning — even as one learns to be more welcoming and more inclusive.

One example of artistic discernment as potentially religious in character comes from an ecumenical video made a number of years ago for the National Conference of Catholic Bishops and entitled *Creativity: Touching the Divine.*[17] When the African-American quilter named

17. *Creativity: Touching the Divine,* United States Catholic Conference, Video 035-4 (1994).

Carole Yvette Lyles talks in that video about her art, she makes an important distinction. There is work of hers that she thinks is good simply because it has an appealing design. It is functional, and it is aesthetically pleasing, but nothing more. There is other work, however, that she feels is more Spirit-filled. In this art she employs special fabrics that she has obtained from Africa and that she, as a Pentecostal Christian, clearly believes help her artistry to glorify God in a special way and to be received as a blessing by her community.

Is this artist's judgment about "spiritual" differences within her own work unwarranted? Does it make too much of the distinction between sacred and secular? These days Christians of all stripes want to break down any artificial wall between the sacred and the secular. African-Americans frequently invoke the holistic spirituality that is said to be typical of the African continent; Catholics invoke the demystifications of Vatican II, embracing a widely sacramental view of life as such; Lutherans talk about the religious calling of all vocations; Presbyterians and other Reformed Christians remind us of how God's claims extend to all arenas of life, including society and state. This erasure of a clear-cut division is salutary in many respects. But in the hands of some, it has led to indiscriminate practices. This is especially true when the conclusion is ventured that every kind of pleasing music (or other art) is fitting for worship, since everything in the world belongs to God and since God blesses every offering that comes from the heart.

This reasoning is flawed. Earth is not yet heaven, the heart is not always pure and undefiled, and not all earthly arts and activities are equally edifying or equally glorifying of God, even when enjoyable. Discernment is necessary. The quilter Carole Yvette Lyles appears to discern perceptively that the Spirit moves more freely and fully through her quilts fabricated with the Pentecostal cross than through her abstract geometrical designs — and not just because they display a cross shape. Whether every viewer would reach the same conclusion is beside the point. The difference is visible, once one is attuned to her medium.

Therefore, the permeability and shifting nature of the divide between sacred and secular is not properly honored simply by asserting that all art is equally worshipful or equally spiritual. Even artists and theologians who affirm the religious core of all true artistry acknowledge that, under the fallen and fallible conditions of human existence, there are major differences. Discernment is as necessary in art as it is in other spheres of life.

Grace in the End, as in the Beginning

The holy cannot be contained or expressed, or even fully acknowledged, by strictly mundane modes of art and expression. Artistic and aesthetic imagination at its highest aspires (however humbly) to reflect and enact a spiritual transformation — a kind of conversion, if you will. That reminds us, however, that, from a Christian perspective, even the highest art, like the lowest, serves worship only by the grace of God, the source of every good and perfect gift. It is with that thought in mind that I offer the remaining chapters of this book, all of which circle around a central issue, like spokes around the hub of a wheel: How to be more inclusive and yet also be more discerning in the practice of arts in and of worship. With the present chapter as a kind of compass, we are prepared to move in the various directions taken in the chapters to come. The art of primary concern here will be music, because that art is virtually omnipresent in worship today and seldom far from controversy. At the same time, each chapter has implications for other arts and for navigating worship and the rest of the Christian life artfully.

CHAPTER 2

Enjoyment and Discernment
in the Music of Worship

Most churchgoers — especially modern churchgoers — want to enjoy worship, not merely endure it. In recent times that desire has doubtless been heightened culturally by the pervasiveness of secular entertainment media such as television and movies, and by the extraordinary popularity of spectator sports. Yet enjoyment seems a fitting part of worship — especially if we recall that, at root, enjoyment means experiencing something with joy, and if we believe (in accordance with seventeenth-century Reformed catechisms) that our ultimate purpose is to glorify and enjoy God. There is also specifically biblical support for enjoyable worship. Christians enthusiastic about "praise choruses" are quick to cite psalms that exhort worshipers to enter the courts of the temple gladly, with praise and thanksgiving.

When it comes to the distinctly enjoyable aspects of worship, the arts play an important role — especially music. But no one these days needs to be told that individuals and entire communities differ greatly with respect to the kinds of art and music they find enjoyable in the context of worship.

Kathleen Norris, for example, speaks for a sometimes vocal but often silently frustrated minority of worshipers in a short piece that appeared a number of years ago in *The Christian Century:*

I find myself saying, "Oh, hell" a lot these days in church. I fully appreciate, as one of the more delicious ironies of the Christian tradition,
that the religion has kept itself alive, has in fact *remained* traditional,
by appropriating and transforming material from the popular culture.
But I often wonder why so many intelligent and well-educated Christians seem to be unable to discern what in our culture might hold possibilities for such scandalous transformation and what is simply
trendy, far too flimsy to stand the weight of time. The problem seems
very deep to me, and far-reaching: I suspect that it originates in the difficulty most of us have in telling good art from bad.[1]

Norris's perspective contrasts strikingly with the broadly inclusive
stance taken by Patrick Kavanaugh in his popular book-length survey
of the history and variety of Christian music. There he pointedly de-
clines to indulge in criticisms of "CCM" (Contemporary Christian
Music) and other popular innovations:

When CCM (among other music) is condemned, it is often attacked on
moral or spiritual grounds: it is called immoral, wrong, harmful, evil,
or even demonic. . . . Such accusations have much more weight than
simply complaining that the music is crummy, inferior, substandard,
mediocre, or just plain awful. Perhaps the most honest parent might
say, "I hate it! I don't know if it's demonic or not, but I can't stand it!"

One could say the same about various types of music — including
every one mentioned in this book — and be perfectly valid. We each
have the right to our individual musical opinions without getting into
the more sensitive area of spiritual judgments. But opinions come and
go, and the corporate opinions of one age are seldom imitated by the
next.[2]

Kavanaugh clearly recognizes and accepts that worshipers will not all
like the same music. What he rejects is the inclination to move from

1. Kathleen Norris, "Sinatra in the Bell Tower," *Christian Century,* March 18-25,
1998, p. 301 (emphasis in the original).
2. Patrick Kavanaugh, *The Music of Angels: A Listener's Guide to Sacred Music
from Chant to Christian Rock* (Chicago: Loyola Press, 1999), pp. 246-47.

aesthetic judgments such as "That music is crummy" to what he terms "spiritual judgments." The latter, presumably, would include Norris's claim that certain kinds of music are not only inferior as art but are also, and perhaps for that very reason, inferior as a means of worship.

My purpose here is not to describe the current state of the ongoing debate regarding arts in worship. Indeed, in some church circles, there is no one left even interested in that debate as formerly carried out. My aim, instead, is to advance the discussion by focusing on the long-term relationship between a set of often-conflicting needs in art and worship: the need for enjoyment, the need for discernment, and the need to negotiate differences in how Christians experience and practice both. Those needs are implicit in the juxtaposition of the two contrasting quotations with which we have begun. Each makes a point worth affirming about church arts and how they are to be judged and enjoyed, but each also fails to discern what the other sees most clearly.

In what follows, I want to avoid an elitist or dogmatic stance, a hint of which is detectable in the Norris quotation cited above. This is a stance that claims to occupy a vantage point from which to identify for everyone's benefit what is good and bad in church artistry, regardless of ecclesial or cultural context. Yet in rejecting aesthetic elitism or dogmatism (which Norris herself objects to in other contexts), I am not denying the need for artistic standards in the sphere of worship, even if these must be flexible and often nonverbal. In fact, I maintain that, unless aesthetic enjoyment in worship does in fact have some perceptible relation to trustworthy discernments that are both artistic and religious, we have no business employing art in worship. In matters of church arts one must eventually (if not immediately) dare to enter into "the more sensitive area of spiritual judgments" — but by way of trying to discern together the spiritual aims and limitations of a given work or style of art, and not by launching personal attacks or by sitting in judgment on people's souls. The following discussion accordingly highlights the importance of discerning the gifts that the arts can bring to worship, and how best to employ and enjoy those gifts.

I am aware of venturing into matters of considerable sensitivity that are by no means easy to sort out — matters that I nonetheless believe to be of vital concern in an era of extensive innovation and renovation in the whole sphere of worship and its arts. By including historical as well as current examples from the sphere of church music, I hope to provide a sense of perspective that is often lost when facing such potentially vexing questions.

Enjoyment of Worship or Enjoyment of Performance

Although worship can be considered a kind of drama, it is not (even when appropriately artful) properly classified as one of "the arts" — certainly not as a "fine art" meant to be appreciated for purely aesthetic reasons. Worship, as everyone claims to realize, is more than an amusing entertainment, a "show," or a performance in the usual sense. Even the most festive or solemn liturgy is something more than an impressive aesthetic display. When the arts enter into worship, they need to be oriented toward communal prayer and praise, and made responsive to word and sacrament.

Nevertheless, the moment an art such as music becomes notably rewarding even as a component of the act of worship, it tends also to become in some sense enjoyable in itself. This tendency of art to give intrinsic delight is one of art's special gifts. Many of us would argue, in fact, that the sheer enjoyment of art can be integral to a blessed life and a flourishing community and, indeed, can provide a foretaste of heavenly bliss. As Nicholas Wolterstorff explains, and as we noted in the previous chapter, art can contribute to *shalom,* a "peace which at its highest is *enjoyment*" — enjoyment of living before God, in nature, and with one's neighbors.[3] Yet this God-given enjoyment of art in its own right or "for its own sake," as we sometimes say (somewhat misleadingly), can introduce a temptation in the context of worship. When a work of liturgical art or music is conspicuously pleasing by virtue of its sheer form or expressivity, not to mention its technical accomplish-

---

3. Nicholas Wolterstorff, *Art in Action: Toward a Christian Aesthetic* (Grand Rapids: William B. Eerdmans, 1980), p. 79.

ment, it may distract the worshiper from attending to the more specifically religious aims of that very art. One could argue, in fact, that one reason why chant has been so readily accommodated to various forms of worship, worldwide, is precisely that chant tends to be self-effacing. One can readily contemplate or pray *through* chant rather than listening *to* chant. Indeed, chant quickly becomes boring when made the focus of strictly aesthetic attention for any extended period of time. Most forms of chant, moreover, offer relatively little opportunity for virtuosic display — which has not altogether prevented chant from being commercially successful, since we have repeatedly seen chant marketed as a spiritually resonant form of "mood" music.

These and other tensions surrounding the enjoyment of the arts in worship are apparent in the repeated (though often soon forgotten) attempts, throughout church history, to discipline and restrain artists, particularly musicians. In 1789, for instance, a convention of Protestant Episcopal bishops, clergy, and laity introduced a new American Prayer Book and an accompanying translation of the book of Psalms. In doing so, they stipulated that every minister should choose which portion of the Psalms would be sung in a given service and, with the possible assistance of "persons skilled in music," should also select suitable tunes. Finally, and especially, it would be the minister's duty "to suppress all light and unseemly music; and all indecency and irreverence in the performance; by which, vain and ungodly persons profane the service of the Sanctuary."[4]

The idea that a minister devoid of musical training should be given primary responsibility for assessing and suppressing all "unseemly" music is inherently problematical, even from a practical point of view. It will come as no surprise that chastening the more talented musicians and finding a fitting use of their art proved difficult. In 1856 the same Episcopal body issued a Pastoral Letter that lamented how choirs were failing by and large to attain the level of "solemnity"

---

4. Reproduced in Jane Rasmussen, *Musical Taste: As a Religious Question in Nineteenth-Century America*, Studies in American Religion, vol. 20 (Lewiston, N.Y.: Edwin Mellen Press, 1986), p. xvii.

characteristic of the "ancient Church." The letter went on to indict practices whereby "the house of prayer is desecrated by a choice of music and a style of performance which are rather suited to the Opera than to the Church — when the organist and the choir seem to be intent only on exciting the admiration of the audience by the display of their artistic skill; and the entertainment of the concert-room is taken as a substitute for the solemn praises of that Almighty Being 'who searcheth the heart.'"[5]

Ostensibly at least, the main problem was just that, again, "organists and choirs are generally allowed to suppose themselves the only proper judges of the subject [of church music], because the Rector is usually no musician." Accordingly, the proposed remedy was to reassert still more strongly that the Rector, while seldom a musician, was nevertheless "better qualified than musicians themselves can be, to decide upon what is suitable to the devotional feelings of the congregation."[6]

As before, one could anticipate a certain amount of difficulty when trying to persuade musicians that a minister untrained in music is really in a position to discern, entirely independently, what sorts of music are most suitable for worship. In any case, there were still other complications to be reckoned with. The stated policy of having the Rector decide on the most suitable music was meant to promote congregational singing above all. This had not always been easy even in the past, however. Certainly it was not easy in the immediately preceding century, when a clerk was often appointed to give out the Psalm tunes and texts to the congregation phrase by phrase, and to lead the responses. Because the clerk might be relatively unmusical, and because this practice of slowly "lining out" the words of each line of a psalm or hymn had its definite aesthetic limitations, the sound of the assembly's voices as they joined together often came closer to dreary murmuring than to singing. The congregation and clergy, far from having been seduced musically into a state of excessive mirth, seemed, in the words of one observer, largely to have for-

5. Rasmussen, *Musical Taste,* p. xix.
6. Rasmussen, *Musical Taste,* p. xx.

gotten that "many of the psalms of David, rehearsed every Sunday, are songs of the triumphant rejoicing."[7]

In the nineteenth century, as the practice of "lining out" faded into the past, and as the role of the clerk was phased out, there was something of a vacuum in the leadership of song-singing. Equally discouraging, from the standpoint of congregational singing, was the intimidation factor introduced by using a trained choir or a professional quartet, who were frequently preoccupied with the intricacies of their art. But even when the congregation was given ample opportunity to sing, many members felt that it was not genteel — but indeed vulgar — to be found singing publicly in church. On many an occasion one could observe "the whole congregation being contented to listen to a mere *performance* of sacred music," as one minister complained.[8] Ministers themselves, however, were often guilty of falling mute during hymns, or of conversing privately while others sang.[9]

Under such circumstances, observers from traditions whose worship tended to be relatively "genteel" and formal were bound to notice that some of the "sects" were better at congregational singing — even if the quality of some of the music was questionable. As one correspondent to the Episcopal periodical the *Churchman* wrote in 1844,

> Congregational music is the music of progress, of advance, of ardent feelings of devotion, and unity in those ardors; and so when we look to the sects that are aggressive we find it prevailing, and sedulously encouraged. The ditties they sing may be worthless as poetry, vile in theological sentiment, and altogether in wretched bad taste, still *the whole congregation is united in singing them.*[10]

---

7. Rasmussen, *Musical Taste,* p. 47.

8. Charles Pettit McIlvaine in a pastoral letter of 1855, quoted in Rasmussen, *Musical Taste,* p. 59 (emphasis in the original).

9. Rasmussen, *Musical Taste,* p. 42.

10. Quoted in Rasmussen, *Musical Taste,* p. 78 (emphasis in the original).

Whither Congregational Singing?

In our day, such observations regarding church music generally, and congregational song in particular, are rarely expressed so bluntly (at least not in public). And they are rightly subject to critical scrutiny when they are. We have become increasingly cautious about embracing the artistic judgments of one social class or educated "elite" and making them absolute and universal. "Wretched bad taste," after all, can come in various forms — including an elitism that dismisses popular arts and tastes as necessarily and thoroughly inferior, even while admiring the enthusiasm behind them. But the question of how to combine enjoyment and discernment in corporate artistry such as congregational singing is both real and persistent.

Much liturgical reform since the Reformation has been designed to give worship and song back to the people. Time and again, liturgists have reacted against excessively professional and performance-oriented musicians, and against trained choirs and organists that have forgotten their primary role as supporters and enablers of the assembly's song. Along the way, worries have cropped up that some church music has been more entertaining than worshipful. But, whereas the "entertaining" music that had most vexed Episcopalian clergy in the nineteenth century was operatic and intricate, the most entertaining worship music in other circles, and particularly in modern times, has derived from popular genres marketed by the entertainment industry. Churches have sought to adopt this music for its broad appeal, in the hopes of "meeting people where they are." That attempt, however, has renewed concerns about mixing secular and sacred values. It has also generated complaints about undue "dumbing down."[11]

Even with all the efforts to encourage congregational singing through popular styles of music, it cannot be said that such singing has

---

11. See Marva J. Dawn, *Reaching Out without Dumbing Down: A Theology of Worship for the Turn-of-the-Century Culture* (Grand Rapids: William B. Eerdmans, 1995). For a more positive "take" on recent trends, see Tex Sample, *The Spectacle of Worship in a Wired World: Electronic Culture and the Gathered People of God* (Nashville: Abingdon Press, 1998).

exactly prospered. At the time of the Second Vatican Council of the 1960s, Protestants and Catholics alike were convinced that it was imperative to make church music more accessible, diverse, and popular in style. Much of the vast treasury of church music was set aside in favor of vernacular and participative music. Many of the folk-style songs and masses produced in the 1960s and 1970s quickly sounded dated, however. And despite the fact that most denominations in subsequent decades created and compiled diverse, international, and mostly singable hymn collections, group singing became less and less popular in the wider culture.

At present, the new technologies of electronic production and digital reproduction have assumed considerable prominence in church — from recorded sound tracks to digital synthesizers, all with the intent of making a contemporary noise to the Lord. Apart from predominantly upbeat contemporary gospel styles, much of the newer music is soft rock or club-style jazz. None of these styles are easily adapted to congregational singing.

"So congregational song is in trouble, nowadays," writes Brian Wren (even while insisting that it is "indispensable"). It is in trouble, he says, not because authority frowns on it, but "because our culture undermines it, through social mobility, performance-oriented popular music, electronic discouragement, and overamplification." Congregational song is further undermined by the fact that, as Wren reports, many children have "no musical background except music videos and TV advertisements."[12] On the Roman Catholic side, Thomas Day offers a long list of related reasons (albeit not always persuasive) as to "why Catholics can't sing."[13]

Without pursuing all these matters in detail, we surely need to

---

12. Brian Wren, *Praying Twice: The Music and Words of Congregational Song* (Louisville: Westminster John Knox Press, 2000), p. 53.

13. Thomas Day, *Why Catholics Can't Sing: The Culture of Catholicism and the Triumph of Bad Taste* (New York: Crossroad, 1990). For a more balanced and in some ways contrary assessment of singing in Catholic contexts (and not only Catholic), see Edward Foley, *Ritual Music: Studies in Liturgical Musicology* (Beltsville, Md.: Pastoral Press, 1995).

pause and pose some basic questions. What kinds of artistic enjoyment really are appropriate for corporate worship? And with whose participation? And in what tradition? Who, after all, should be deciding? It seems we need to be thinking much more deeply and clearly about what it means to use arts in worship. That means trying to understand more fully what distinguishes those arts and media among themselves, and what distinguishes artistic gifts from others brought to worship. How would we change our picture of the possible gifts and roles of music and other arts in worship if we were to take seriously their special and distinctive powers of creation, proclamation, and imagination?

It would be surprising if these large and complex questions could be answered altogether satisfactorily by any worship committee at present, or by any school of theology, let alone by any one liturgist or theologian. Yet they are being put on the docket, so to speak. In the remaining pages, we can hope to make some progress in addressing several of them if we return to the issues of enjoyment and discernment raised by the examples we have already cited.

Catering to the Comfortable

What kinds of enjoyment in worship are appropriately Christian? An assumption evidently shared by both Kathleen Norris and the nineteenth-century Episcopal bishops — and by countless other Christians, in fact — is that, fundamentally, worship is serious business. That is why Norris speaks of the inadequacies of "flimsy" church arts as a "deep problem" — sometimes amusing in a way, but basically no laughing matter. Again, the Episcopal Bishops' Pastoral Letter of 1856, when it calls for a certain "solemnity" in church singing, treats the matter seriously by warning that trivial music desecrates the house of prayer. In keeping with that spirit, the earlier rubric for the new Prayer Book (1789) had wanted to suppress all "light and unseemly music" as profane and irreverent and had condemned the practitioners of such music as ungodly.

Those earlier stern rebukes of lightly entertaining forms of church music sound almost quaint in an era that prides itself on cultivating tolerance. They come from an era in American history in which, according to Mark Noll, Americans seemed, whatever their formal religious beliefs, "to retain a generally sober, even Calvinistic, view of humanity, concerned much more with human limitations than with human potential."[14] Today we are more conscious that seriousness can be overdone and that some of the legitimate variety in Christian music extends, as Kavanaugh points out, to music that is distinctly loud and lively and that in some settings would seem irreverent. Some of the music that clergy of the nineteenth century approved as appropriately serious and restrained has come to seem to us exceedingly bland and dull, even "flimsy." By contrast, much of the Christian and otherwise religious music from Hispanic contexts, for example, or from Africa and the African diaspora, is full of melodic verve and rhythmic vitality.

Thus, it seems plain that some of the fundamentally serious aims of worship can be served by music that is openly more entertaining and more animated than that traditionally sanctioned in many (though not all) of the European and Euro-American traditions. One reason could be this: Human beings come only with difficulty to any significant time of turning and transformation. We need to be wooed and won over. The art of worship music, when enjoyable, can soften the heart and motivate the will, as Calvin himself knew well even if he would have objected to anything smacking of worldly entertainment. In addition, some music that is relatively easy and light can help create a sense of community. Whereas Calvinist churches during the Reformation era had disciplined the worshiping community's enjoyment through an austere form of unaccompanied, unison Psalm-singing, their descendants today have developed a greater appreciation of the legitimate role of lively, rhythmic, and heartwarming music in drawing the worshiper into Christian communion and mutual commitment.[15]

14. Mark A. Noll, *A History of Christianity in the United States and Canada* (Grand Rapids: William B. Eerdmans, 1992), p. 229.

15. See, for instance, the chapter on contemporary worship music in Brian Wren, *Praying Twice*, pp. 127-66.

At the same time, everyone realizes at some level that, from a Christian perspective, life is no joke; neither is the search for justice and holiness. Those who are most appreciative of the searching, soulful powers of art and music often find themselves wondering, therefore, why Christians seem so willing to consign music to the role of a relatively undemanding, "feel-good" medium. One wonders how healthy it is that so little popular music today in a gospel style or from Latin America draws on vernacular traditions that include lament and yearning or protest: spirituals and flamenco, for instance. Even those youth who supposedly are turned off by musical seriousness sometimes remark that the church likes to take up popular music at its most sanitized and innocuous. The 2001 season finale of the television series *The West Wing* made haunting use of the now-classic rock song "Brothers in Arms" by the group Dire Straits. That song, while not something most listeners would think of as "cutting edge," can be heard as musically far more serious than most of what one hears in suburban megachurches. Why churches tend to avoid the more searching kinds of art and music even when adopting popular styles is thus a pressing question. Some of the reasons may be theological, such as a widespread fixation on a kind of "prosperity Gospel" that in effect denies the place of mourning or spiritual thirst. One might suspect that another reason, more strictly musical, is that many worship leaders have so little idea what music and other art is capable of, beyond a customary comfort zone — and relatively little awareness of why it could be worth their while to find out.

It should at least give us pause that certain affluent, comfortable suburban churches are among those currently preoccupied with singing simple praise and worship choruses — choruses that, while sometimes able to serve graciously to comfort the afflicted, also tend to lift the heart without searching it. Similarly, it seems fair to ask why so many churches of economically cushioned Americans are infusing their easygoing worship with soft rock and club-style jazz, and thus with music that is normally associated with the lightest and least responsible moments in life. Might it not be possible that they are replicating in a different way the earlier predilection of affluent and high-status churches for relatively sophisticated but anodyne kinds of music safely removed from life's harder realities and grander joys? At the same time, those in more traditional, "mainline" churches might do well to ask whether their frequent reluctance to venture far from long-established genres of church music and art isn't conditioned by social and intellectual biases and by potentially unhealthy tendencies toward complacency.

Cultivating Aesthetic Judgments for Worship

At this point, of course, we are no longer talking just about the kind of enjoyment and level of seriousness we are to seek in the arts of worship. We are also attempting to discern the place and importance of artistic substance and quality, which is admittedly something that musicians and other artists are far more likely to consider important than clergy are. Yet it is just here, in considering how to discern artistic quality and its place in the church, that the issues become most slippery. One recalls, for instance, Kavanaugh's point that almost every form of music, whatever its particular assets, seems vulnerable to *some* form of criticism. Music lovers and theologians alike have long lamented the sentimentality of many Victorian hymns. Others have complained about the formal complexity and emotional coolness of Renaissance polyphony, the unintelligibility of the words in Baroque counterpoint, the "vain repetitions" of antiphonal responses, the excessive otherworldliness of Gregorian chant, and so forth.

Those judgments are often incompatible with each other. One reason is that perceptions regarding any church art take place partly in relation to a particular tradition, which has its own possibilities and expectations. A Hammond organ with timbres that would destroy the awe-inspiring sound of Messiaen's *Livre du Saint Sacrement* (1984) can lend essential vitality and vibrancy to much gospel music. The expectations that come with a tradition can take surprising shapes, moreover. In a Presbyterian church that has customarily excluded all visual art, the introduction of pious paintings or figurative sculpture might seem heretical or at least faintly idolatrous to those very same worshipers who presently welcome video film clips projected onto screens in strategic locations around the worship space — or who, when they find themselves invited to Catholic worship, can sometimes feel blessed by the surrounding sculptures and paintings of biblical figures and saints.

The conflict between various norms for church art is not due only to the ways in which traditions shape our expectations and responses. It is also due to the fact that we necessarily mix various kinds of criteria when assessing church art and music — from theological criteria ("God requires words in order to talk to us, even through music") to more aesthetic criteria ("The beauty of polyphony is more impersonal and elevated than that of hymn tunes"). When various criteria come into play, not everyone will agree on which factors are more important. For listeners attuned to the spiritual import of the beauty of Renaissance polyphony, for instance, the Council of Trent's complaints about the unintelligibility of sacred words in complex polyphonic settings seem somewhat misplaced, at least to the extent that they ignore how the quality of the beauty of the music itself can mediate a sense of the divine. Words might not always need to take precedence in the arts of the church if one happens to believe, with various theologians, that all beauty — all aesthetic goodness — is from God, and honors God.[16]

Yet even that general principle about the holiness of beauty must be qualified, and significantly so. For it remains the case that beauties vary enormously in kind, and that music that is good in some contexts is not always good for worship. In the eighteenth century, for instance, members of the clergy in Austria had some liturgical justification for worrying about the more florid sections of Mozart's masses, which would have raised no questions in the context of his operas.

Indeed, as we will have opportunity to note on more than one occasion — and much to the chagrin of aesthetes whose primary approach to holiness is through supreme beauty and artistic excellence — music

16. For an extended discussion of beauty as a "transcendental" that is found to some degree in everything that so much as exists, and is ultimately divine in origin and goal, see Richard Viladesau, *Theological Aesthetics: God in Imagination, Beauty, and Art* (New York: Oxford University Press, 1999).

and art that is somewhat flawed or inferior can actually be good for worship, and sometimes better than art that is more polished. The "fuguing tunes" of William Billings and other American composers of the eighteenth century sound somewhat crude to ears trained on subtleties of musical counterpoint and voice-leading. But the very crudeness of the writing somehow contributes to a sense of sturdy faith and of a religious vigor suitable to the New World.

One might conclude from the abundance of aesthetically questionable art in church that whatever aesthetic criteria are appropriate to judging church arts must be very different from the criteria used in judging secular arts. Andrew Sullivan, a Roman Catholic and former editor of the *New Republic,* once went so far as to declare in an interview that the very "tackiness" of the church is testimony to something greater working through it, and a sign of the power of the truth that survives the institution.[17] There is no denying that Christian aesthetic discernment cannot simply be equated with conventional good taste or with "worldly" artistic standards even at their highest.

But that is not the end of the matter. A similar thing can be said, after all, regarding reasoning in theology as compared with reasoning in secular philosophy. Although it may be that the religious heart has reasons unknown to the philosophical head, every theologian employs certain strategies of sound reasoning found also in "worldly" philosophy; and many theologians (such as Augustine and Thomas Aquinas) have been deeply informed by wisdom gleaned from non-Christian philosophy. Similarly, even "worldly" aesthetics can be relevant to church arts. In their arts, Christians explore and express certain realities that are invisible from some secular standpoints. But Christian worship suffers when the resources of secular arts are simply neglected.

And that has happened all too often. The sad fact is that, for several centuries now, the church has rarely made full and "inspired" use of the arts at their best. Accordingly, since the eighteenth century, the most creative artistry (including religious artistry) has tended to take

17. Bob Roehr, "Cheap Shots: A Talk with Andrew Sullivan," *Christian Century,* Sept. 13-29, 1995, p. 5.

place outside the church. Christians may need to find out anew, therefore, what all art can do, and to discover again the religious value of deep and substantial works of art in a variety of styles.

As Christians rediscover what the arts can do in and for worship, and as artists rediscover their spiritual and liturgical roots, we may need to find worship venues that can allow artistic forms room to develop and grow. In the mid-eighteenth century, Bach's weekly Sunday cantatas occupied at least twenty minutes prior to the sermon; on occasion a second cantata was sung at the time of communion as well. That cantata music, most musicians agree, was great from both a religious and an aesthetic standpoint — even if such cantatas themselves sometimes encountered objections that they were too operatic and theatrical. We can yearn to recover a place for such liturgical art or to develop modern counterparts. But we must realize that the Lutheran morning service, at least in Leipzig, lasted approximately three hours, with the sermon alone taking an hour of that time. If we do not want to endure a liturgy of that length simply to accommodate various kinds of worship music at their most developed, we might do well to provide, on a regular basis, alternative occasions for art (both ancient and modern) to stretch its wings within the life of the church.

One can treat church arts as "adiaphora," in the sense that little about the arts of worship has been prescribed scripturally. But that is true of almost any specific feature of worship itself. The fact remains that art can be vital to worship, and uniquely so. When a work or style is excluded from the church due to a failure to discern its potential for worship, that can be a significant loss for the church as well as for the arts. Even though the Austrian clergy had a point in worrying about the operatic sounds of Mozart's youthful masses composed for Salzburg Cathedral, musicians have long recognized what the clergy missed: the almost miraculous capacity of Mozart's music to transcend the conventional limitations of the classical Austrian mass — particularly (and ironically) in daringly "operatic" passages in a work such as the Mass in C Minor. In retrospect, modern theologians such as Karl Barth and Hans Küng have glimpsed traces of transcendence in Mozart's music and have heard in it parables of gospel tidings, because the music itself conveys in a uniquely artistic manner a sense of joy that knows and overcomes despair.[18] That was not noticed so keenly by theologians and clergy at the time, so far as we know.

The importance of artistic discernment can be seen in humbler settings as well, as can been observed in an example familiar from our own hymnals. Most church musicians would agree that the hymn tunes of Ralph Vaughan Williams are musically substantial and beautifully shaped, with harmonies that unite the fresh with the traditional. It would make no sense to claim that the religious value of "For All the Saints" and "Come Down, O Love Divine" is unrelated to the intrinsic aesthetic qualities of the music. On the contrary, the music (despite Vaughan Williams's private inclinations toward agnosticism) conveys a quite exceptional sense of spiritual movement and divine engagement; and the marriage of words and music in these hymns is so happy that one could only wish it were achieved more often.

Such considerations regarding the potential religious importance of musical excellence were surely in the mind of Vaughan Williams himself, as musical editor of the *English Hymnal* (1906 and 1933), when he argued that many of the then-popular hymn tunes were so inferior and sentimental as to be "positively harmful" to those singing them in church. While wanting to qualify that assertion in all sorts of ways, we might do well to listen when Vaughan Williams declares, "It ought no longer to be true anywhere that the most exalted moments of a church-goer's week are associated with music that would not be tolerated in any place of secular entertainment."[19] This is approximately the same point that Kathleen Norris makes when complaining about the "flimsy" and faddish quality of so much art being welcomed into the church.

18. See Karl Barth, *Wolfgang Amadeus Mozart,* trans. Clarence K. Pott (Grand Rapids: William B. Eerdmans, 1986); and Hans Küng, *Mozart: Traces of Transcendence,* trans. John Bowden (Grand Rapids: William B. Eerdmans, 1993).

19. Ralph Vaughan Williams, "The Music," from a preface to the *English Hymnal* (1906), 2d ed. (London: Oxford University Press, 1933), p. ix.

Reforming Art and Music for the Church

I have been arguing that the discernment of quality and appropriateness (or lack thereof) is both legitimate and important in relation to the arts of the church. Such discernment is best a product of joint effort, and needs always to take into account different cultural and congregational contexts.

As we have seen, the need for a communal exercise of discernment is particularly great when venturing into new artistic territory in the realm of worship. Then, especially, the basic choices cannot wisely be left to musicians alone, or only to clergy, or to mono-cultural worship committees. Clergy and non-artists left to themselves will often banish the most creative and searching art from the church, assuming it to be too difficult or too entertaining, too serious or not serious enough. Musicians left to themselves will too often choose a certain work of music simply because it is fun to play or musically interesting — regardless of whether it is meant to provide support for communion or interpret the biblical text for the day.

In any case, it is crucial to take into account the discernments of Christians and others who are actively involved in the arts. They are the ones most likely to sense the religious potential of an art form that could otherwise seem overly "entertaining" or virtuosic or secular. This is so, even if they need to be reminded from time to time that almost any style of new music or art — such as liturgical dance — needs gradual and informative introduction in church. Such art commonly comes across as "secular," or as a mere "performance," until worshipers become familiar with its language.

There is another reason for churches to attend especially to the discernments of the more artistically trained and attuned. Every art, insofar as it is aesthetic, is distinctive as art primarily because its message is embodied in its medium. An artistic form is never just the "package" that conveys a religious message. Instead, the artistic form invariably shapes the sense of the message itself. In the case of music, nothing one can say in words can exhaust the meanings and enjoyments music conveys, or can explain fully the sense of things its artful

43

sounds can bring into being. At times, music may be relatively neutral with respect to the religious (or secular) meanings with which it is compatible. The same hymn tune can sometimes provide a satisfactory medium for very different sets of words. And that one tune can in fact be sung differently in different settings — factors which help explain the successful importation of secular melodies into sacred contexts. There is no one-to-one correspondence between a particular musical (or other artistic) "idea" and a specific religious concept. No chord progression or other musical pattern invariably "means" the Trinity, for instance, though Bach found many musical devices to symbolize Trinitarian divinity. The conceptual ambiguity of music hardly means that worshipers need not try to discern the specific character of the music they hear or sing. In fact, the intrinsic power and inexplicable "meaning" of music should cause worshipers to listen even more carefully to music's inner voice so as to discern how each kind or work of music enters and forms hearts and minds. The range of possibilities may be broad. But it remains the case that some music tends to invite amusement and diversion; other music asks us to follow it deeper or higher — and to discipline ourselves to do so, if we are not yet ready.

Bringing the discernments of artists and worship leaders together is particularly important in view of the fact that, as I have pointed out, much of the most spiritually exploratory and aesthetically compelling artistry since the seventeenth or early eighteenth century has developed outside the church. Artists and musicians in the secular world, whether working in classical styles or vernacular, have discovered formal and expressive resources that the church has barely glimpsed up to now. In doing so, they have sometimes challenged commonly accepted religious beliefs, moral values, and modes of expression. One thinks of the symphonies of Gustav Mahler or the paintings of the abstract expressionists, or popular songs by the Indigo Girls or Sweet Honey in the Rock — not to mention a large number of contemporary films. Such artistry can be valuable to the church itself, but it cannot necessarily be imported directly and uncritically into worship. It seems almost inevitable that artistic styles that have long been tailored to the requirements of secular culture will need reforming before they will fit certain crucial needs of worship.

The risks of uncritically appropriating secular styles can be especially great when the church seeks out accessible music and media that it hopes will be attractive to youthful newcomers. Suppose, for example, that we in fact live in a society that consumes amusements at a rate never before seen in history. Suppose that Neil Postman has a point, therefore, when he argues that we are "amusing ourselves to death."[20] Suppose, moreover, that the major entertainment corporations, the "merchants of cool," invest almost unimaginable quantities of money in researching and marketing to a teen culture that has more wealth and independence than ever before.[21] Suppose, finally, that there is a genuine if elusive connection between the kind of music being marketed most widely and the morally questionable goods being sold most aggressively. It should be evident, then, why the wholesale adoption and "baptism" of commercially popular music and media for the purposes of luring youth and newcomers to church can be risky business. This is not to deny an important — even key — role for popular music in church. But if popular (and other) artists are to bring their gifts to the house of worship, both they and the leaders of worship will need to exert considerable effort to discover what is appropriate.

It is worth pointing out, in this connection, that a willingness to engage freshly and creatively in artistry in the context of worship is sometimes easier to cultivate in amateur artists than in professionals (whether popular or "elite"). To be sure, churches need to be more aware than ever of the special gifts that professional artists can bring. But professional artists sometimes have too much at stake in their preconceptions of their art — preconceptions usually formed, these days, far from any church or religious setting. There were good aesthetic reasons why the Italian filmmaker Pier Paolo Pasolini, when directing the highly acclaimed *Gospel According to St. Matthew* (1964), used a

20. Neil Postman, *Amusing Ourselves to Death: Public Discourse in the Age of Show Business* (New York: Penguin, 1986).

21. See *The Merchants of Cool*, Frontline, PBS Video FROL-1909 (Spring 2001).

number of local Italian villagers in leading parts, and his own mother as the Virgin Mary. Professional actors would likely have had to unlearn too much.

Where does this leave us? It should be abundantly clear that the joy and enjoyment in worship can be enhanced through artistry — both as an offering to God and as an offering to the community, an offering to be enjoyed "in God." If our theologies and spiritualities are to be embodied, we have ample reason to discern and affirm the delightful and imaginative qualities of sensory (rather than sensational) artistry as a medium of worship — a medium not to be denied or circumscribed by an overly narrow concept of either word or sacrament, but affirmed in relation to both.

If others do not discern as we do, we may be tempted, like Kathleen Norris in our earlier example, to become impatient, possibly applying our own hard-won convictions a little too confidently and defensively. Or else we may be tempted, like Patrick Kavanaugh, to give up trying to connect artistic and religious criteria at all, thereby blessing everything indiscriminately. Neither of those approaches satisfies for long. Worship leaders and artists need, most of all, to ground themselves theologically and artistically — and then to stretch. As in other spheres, this becomes a matter of critical correlation and communal reflection. We need continually to discern what promises to respond, artistically and creatively, to newly disclosed aims of biblically rooted worship in which we were formed and to which Christians believe themselves to be called. And we need to discern what promises to respond, liturgically, to the resources of religiously enlivening arts that we have newly discovered or newly recovered. Our stance will need to be pluralistic, therefore — but critical.

Taking such an approach, we can hope (indeed, can anticipate) that enjoyment and discernment will join together in worship. That will be needed in a time marked by the creation of new modes of art, by the recreation of classic and traditional arts worldwide, and by the combined activity of artists and religious communities as they pursue in often unpredictable ways an array of goals they discover they share in common, by the grace of God.

CHAPTER 3

Singing Together
(with All Creation):
Dilemmas and Delights

Canticle

Most of us have noticed that, on those rare occasions when people from various parts of the world come together and sing, the boundaries that normally confine and define us can suddenly seem to blur or even to disappear. At such times we may have experienced the joy-filled communal singing as a foretaste of the celestial banquet — the heavenly feast that will include, at one glorious meal, the redeemed from every place and time. In that kind of experience, distinctions of class and nationality, of race and gender, no longer separate us. Our voices express our common participation in the life of God.

The famous canticle that Saint Francis composed in the thirteenth century, during a severe illness near the end of his life, invokes communal singing at its most expansive and encompassing. Translated into English by William Draper as "All Creatures of Our God and King," the original canticle celebrates the singing of all creation, and the communion of all things in God. Saint Francis, using vernacular Italian (in the Umbrian dialect), exhorts the praise of God with *(cum)* and through *(per)* all created things — Brother Sun above all, and secondarily Sister Moon, but also Brother Wind and Sister Water, and Brother Fire and Sister Earth, and so on. Francis addresses the words of his song directly to

God: *"Altissimu, omnipotente bonsignore"* — "Exalted, most powerful Lord . . ./May you be praised with all your creations, especially Brother Sun; . . ./May you be praised through Sister Moon and the stars."

Draper's English rendition from 1925 — commonly sung to Vaughan Williams's arrangement of the tune "Lasst uns erfreuen" — differs from the original in that it no longer addresses God directly but, rather, addresses the creatures and creations of God: "All creatures of our God and King,/Lift up your voice and with us sing,/O praise ye! Alleluia!" It is a small change. Draper's translation follows the pattern of Psalm 148, which Francis also must have had in mind. And Draper's version remains in the spirit of Francis, who preached to the birds and made friends with a predatory wolf. But by addressing the creatures of God and asking them to join us in singing God's praise, Draper's translation generates a question less likely to be raised by the original canticle: When we exhort all of God's diverse peoples and creatures to praise God, how could they possibly understand us? After all, we are using our own language, not theirs.

The mere fact that God's created beings use very different languages in prayer and praise is presumably no problem for God, of course. We can safely assume that God, who is said to know all of us better than we know ourselves, has no personal need of translators. The problem is ours. The very moment we tell the whole world we want to praise God together, we must necessarily rely on our own language, culture, and concept of God.[1] But that may be alienating rather than inviting, and it threatens to undercut the experience we are most hoping to share — the experience of being united in praise of God. How can we even know whether we are all praising the same God, given that we are speaking different languages and may have rather different ideas of God to begin with?

1. For a recent if challenging discussion of the importance of culture in the context of theology, see Kathryn Tanner, *Theories of Culture: A New Agenda for Theology* (Minneapolis: Augsburg Fortress Press, 1997). The general problem of cultural translation is addressed in suggestive ways in the essays collected in *The Translatability of Cultures: Figurations of the Space Between,* ed. Sanford Budick and Wolfgang Iser (Stanford, Calif.: Stanford University Press, 1996).

This is not a puzzle or frustration that is likely to occur to anyone in the midst of singing either the original canticle or its English translation. But the dilemma I have identified is, unfortunately, all too real in the everyday world. What is troubling is that the very words and songs we employ in order to invite others into worship and into communal harmony often end up creating a sense of difference and division between us. The very way we express ourselves, even among Christians, may undercut the message we want to transmit. That is quite apart from the fact that, in some instances, no matter which language or mode of expression we choose, certain other people will reject it as inadequate or inappropriate.

Disharmony

Let me bring the problem a bit closer to home. Is it not the case these days that the songs we ourselves most want to share in worship are sometimes the very songs that are least welcomed by many of our brothers and sisters in Christ? And are we not pained when others find our most treasured songs boring or jarring or otherwise objectionable? As the philosopher Immanuel Kant pointed out long ago, part of the experience of beauty is our sense that genuine beauty transcends our private perception. Even though we realize that the perception of beauty takes place subjectively, we feel that something we perceive to be beautiful should be enjoyed by others (if not necessarily universally, as Kant himself thought).[2] Theologians have even been known to declare that beauty has its ultimate source and goal in God, the creator of us all.[3] How ironic and troubling, then, that we often have such

2. For a discussion of the whole topic of conflicts and confluences of aesthetic judgment in the religious sphere, see Frank Burch Brown, *Good Taste, Bad Taste, and Christian Taste: Aesthetics in Religious Life* (New York: Oxford University Press, 2000).

3. Among the more cogent of the relatively recent treatments of beauty and divinity are Edward Farley, *Faith and Beauty: A Theological Aesthetic* (Burlington, Vt.: Ashgate, 2001); Richard Harries, *Art and the Beauty of God* (New York: Mowbray, 1993); Patrick Sherry, *Spirit and Beauty*, 2d ed. (London: SCM, 2002); and David Bentley

trouble sharing the very things that we find most beautiful and holy, and therefore most *worth* sharing!

One difficulty we encounter in trying to share our songs has to do with what theologians call finitude. We are necessarily limited by being individual creatures living in circumscribed communities, all with distinctive languages and cultures. But there is another difficulty, which has more to do with what we might as well call sin. As I have already noted, on special occasions we have the exhilarating experience of joining together with a multitude of diverse voices, harmoniously singing the praise of God. In church and in the world we daily confront a harsher, more dissonant reality, however. We hear voices that are raised in conflict, hostility, and mutual accusation, or voices lowered in stunned fear and stark terror. We witness voices silenced unduly by shame or oppression. We also discover that singing itself, which can be among the most harmonious of activities, can be aggressive and invasive — even in nature, as when birds stake out nesting territory. In a previous era, Catholics complained that Lutherans were using music to lure followers into hell. In France, Huguenots and Catholics each sang their own Christian battle songs as they prepared for military conflict with each other. In churches today, songs labeled "contemporary" and "traditional" are likewise lifted as battle banners in the "worship wars."

Of course it is not just singing that concerns us, but singing as part of the larger process of cultural interaction, which is fraught with conflict as well as with the potential for growth and gladness. Issues of encounter and meaningful communication between different identities and communities are among the most pressing issues of our time. They affect everything we do. They have to do with whether we will thrive or even survive. In many ways we benefit as the world shrinks from the effects of high-speed transportation, electronic and digital communication, global commerce, and religious and political exchange. The resulting emergence of one diverse global village creates an exciting

Hart, *The Beauty of the Infinite: The Aesthetics of Christian Truth* (Grand Rapids: William B. Eerdmans, 2003).

prospect of a culturally and spiritually richer life for all of us. But none of us can be unaware that a "shrinking" world such as ours can be frightening, too. As diverse cultures come into closer and closer contact, there is at least an initial stage of greater risk. We risk misunderstanding, exploitation, and conflict. Even the power to communicate can easily degenerate into the power to control and dominate, or else to sabotage and terrorize. The story of the Tower of Babel makes it plain that merely being able to talk the same language does not guarantee a perfect world.

I began by invoking the canticle composed by Francis of Assisi. I opened with that canticle's concern for the singing of all creation because I believe that, in an era in which every group is understandably asserting its own identity and voice, we also need to cultivate a vision of the larger religious purpose of congregational music. We need to keep in mind the truly transformative song to which God invites us to contribute, all in different ways and possibly in different styles and languages. But I noted that sharing songs collectively is not just a simple matter of inviting everyone to participate, without attending to matters of culture and context. Accordingly, I want now to focus on two related matters pertinent specifically to the challenge of diverse peoples joining in songs of worship together: first, the idea of translation as mediating difference, and of poetry and music as providing especially effective means of translating the gospel across those lines of difference; and second, the importance of what I like to call "ecumenical taste" to such transmission and translation.

Translating Faith into Song

The American poet Robert Frost once remarked that poetry is what gets lost in translation. Every translation is imperfect, especially when it involves poetry. (I have found that humor is also often lost in translation.) Be that as it may, Hebrew and Greek Scriptures — from the Psalms to the book of Revelation — assure us that the inevitable imperfection of every human translation of the divine song is no cause for final despair. The linguistic and cultural differences that remain between us need not ultimately divide. We should not forget that an eventual remedy for the confusion of tongues associated with the fall of the Tower of Babel was signified by the Day of Pentecost. On that occasion people from many nations were all amazed to hear the apostles' message in their own native language.

But what if we were to take seriously the idea that one thing vital to faith and to religious expression is, indeed, the *poetry* of religion, and the *music* of faith? I don't mean this only in a metaphorical sense. I am asking what difference it would make if we were convinced that part of what is at the heart of faith really is best embodied and transmitted artistically and aesthetically — in poetry and story and song?[4] Genesis is filled with artful storytelling. The Psalms and the book of Job are wonderful poetry.[5] Jesus taught through the verbal art of the parables. The hymns of the church resound with what is distinctive and enlivening about Christian faith.

One can take this line of thought too far, to be sure. Art can sometimes be used as a substitute for religion rather than treated as one part of religious life and practice. In the eighteenth century, Alexander Pope, in his *Essay on Criticism*, wittily observed, "Some to the church repair/Not for the doctrine but for the music there." Nevertheless — and this is my main point here — when church music is practiced well, one is not actually being unfaithful to come to church to hear the music! The music, among other things, may well provide a "translation" and interpretation of the meaning of Scripture and doctrine, becoming what Charles and John Wesley termed an exercise in "practical divinity."[6] Our songs really do give voice to, and participate in, God's work of creation and redemption. Thus, poetry and music, when combined

4. See Paul Mariani, *God and the Imagination: On Poets, Poetry, and the Ineffable* (Athens, Ga.: University of Georgia Press, 2002); and Nathan A. Scott Jr., *The Poetics of Belief* (Chapel Hill: University of North Carolina Press, 1985).

5. See Robert Alter, *The Art of Biblical Poetry* (New York: Basic Books, 1985).

6. From the preface to the 1780 hymnbook *John and Charles Wesley: Selected Prayers, Hymns, Journal Notes, Sermons, Letters, and Treatises*, ed. Frank Whaling (New York: Paulist Press, 1981), p. 176.

in the act of singing, are not just the frosting on the cake of worship, but integral to the practice of worship.[7] Religious proclamation and presence rely on, and indeed generate, what philosophers such as Paul Ricoeur call a "surplus of meaning," which is native to the language of art, symbol, and metaphor.[8]

You might say that this is something we've always known. Luther, and indeed Calvin, had high praise for musical worship as one of the greatest of God's gifts. So did many nineteenth-century revivalists. But many theologians and ministers have had difficulty figuring out the overall value and place of music in the Christian life. So-called mainline Protestant seminaries have seldom required their ministerial students to have any extensive knowledge of church music and hymnody. And in some evangelical circles, it has been common to treat hymns and gospel songs as spiritual warm-up exercises before the sermon, or as colorful musical packages in which to deliver gospel truth.

Again, what if we considered religious arts such as congregational song differently? What if we really embraced the idea that song can provide a gracious way of translating the meaning of faith in such a way as to mediate the radical difference both between God and ourselves, and between us as human beings, not least by addressing body and mind and heart together? I have already suggested that quite the opposite can occur. But, under the right circumstances, the very act of singing recalls the first Christian Pentecost and anticipates, as well, the heavenly banquet. Although the poetry of faith can sometimes get lost in translation, and especially in prose translation, a truly musical translation of the poetry of faith can bring the meaning and motivation of faith to life. On this view, congregational

7. See, for instance, Don Saliers, "Singing Our Lives," in *Practicing Our Faith*, ed. Dorothy C. Bass (San Francisco: Jossey-Bass, 1997).

8. See Paul Ricoeur, *Interpretation Theory: Discourse and the Surplus of Meaning* (Fort Worth: Texas Christian University Press, 1976). See also the exploration of the explicitly religious implications in Part One of Paul Ricoeur, *Figuring the Sacred: Religion, Narrative, and Imagination*, trans. David Pellauer, ed. Mark I. Wallace (Minneapolis: Fortress Press, 1995), pp. 35-72.

song at its best both interprets (as proclamation) and enacts (in a sacramental way) what it means to be the body of Christ in the world. Is this not consistent with the self-understanding of many hymns themselves?

The Wide Reach of Singing

It is one thing to hear theologians and preachers talk about congregational song; it is another to turn to songs themselves for a sense of their own vocation. It is worth remarking how many hymns picture the actual singing of diverse people and creatures as both a symbol and an embodiment of a divinely blessed community. Alluding to Psalm 148 (in the manner of Saint Francis), one familiar English hymn exhorts, "Let the whole creation cry, 'Alleluia.'" We likewise have George Herbert's "Let All the World in Every Corner Sing." And there is the classic William Kethe versification of Psalm 100, which has traditionally been sung to the tune "Old Hundredth": "All people that on earth do dwell,/Sing to the Lord with cheerful voice;/Him serve with mirth, his praise forth tell,/Come ye before him and rejoice."

Still other hymns conjure up an image of multivoiced, blended singing by borrowing not from the Psalms but from the book of Revelation. Many of these hymns ask us to imagine coming into the heavenly Zion and singing around the throne of God. As one such hymn puts it, "We're marching to Zion — beautiful, beautiful Zion." The beloved early American folk hymn "Wondrous Love" cries out, "To God and to the Lamb/I will sing, I will sing . . ./To God and to the Lamb/Who is the great 'I Am,'/While millions join the theme, I will sing. . . ."

We should take notice, too, of a superlative hymn of recent origin — namely, Carl Daw's "As Newborn Stars Were Stirred to Song." The text, alluding to biblical passages from Exodus and Job to Matthew and Mark, describes how music bursts forth in all times and places, awakening awe and gratitude, and giving faith a voice. It opens this way: "As newborn stars were stirred to song when all things came to be,/as Miriam and Moses sang when Israel was set free,/so music bursts unbidden forth when God-filled hearts rejoice,/to waken awe and gratitude and give mute faith a voice."[9]

All of these congregational songs attempt to reach out across all actual and potential divisions partly by using words, of course. But the words they use refer to singing, to music.

I think it is no accident that many poems that aspire to a virtually universal scope are intended to be sung — to be set to music. On a rather mundane level, some of us might remember the Coke ad from many years ago in which youthful singers beamed out, "I'd love to teach the world to sing in perfect harmony." The song ended by offering us Coke as the "Real Thing." On a much more elevated artistic level, we have Schiller's *An die Freude* — the "Ode to Joy" that Beethoven set in the final movement of the Ninth Symphony. That ode is certainly meant for singing, and it is plainly addressed to the whole of humanity: *Seid umschlungen, Millionen!/Diesen Kuss der ganzen Welt!*: "Be embraced, you millions!/This kiss is for the entire world!"

Apparently when we human beings want our words to reach out as far as possible, and so to be transmitted and translated to the world at large, we turn to song — that is, to words and music together. To be sure, music by itself can sometimes reach even farther. But music alone is ambiguous in some respects (even if precise in others). Music without words could never convey, by itself, the full meaning of the gospel, because music alone is not referential and conceptual in the manner of language. But there is a sense in which words alone lack something music and poetry supply. Thus, when combined with words, or when heard in a worship setting that orients the listening process, music opens up a vital sense of the "felt" significance of the text. Singing takes hold of the body and the imagination, of the heart as well as the head. That is one of the great gifts of art, and a special gift of song.

9. Carl Daw, "As Newborn Stars Were Stirred to Song," in *Wonder, Love, and Praise: A Supplement to the [Episcopal] Hymnal 1982* (New York: Church Pension Fund, 1997), #788.

Cultural Reconsiderations

Earlier we touched on some hard facts about the way in which the songs we love may be resisted or rejected. We noted that singing is not always inclusive and benign, that it can also be exclusive and aggressive. So perhaps we had better not get carried away with the transcendent element in congregational song. We need to come back down to earth.

It is hard to think of a hymn or song that cannot be criticized from some legitimate point of view by people in another cultural situation or social location. The "Canticle" that Saint Francis wrote appears in some hymnbooks these days without any reference to the sun as brother or to the moon as sister, and without speaking of fire as brother or of water as sister. Some Christians today find the original language of "brother" and "sister" to be too sexist and, in that context, too hierarchical. One new adaptation of William Kethe's metrical version of Psalm 100 renders the first line as "All people that on earth do dwell/Sing out your faith with cheerful voice," instead of "Sing to the Lord with cheerful voice." That way the deity is not identified as a male ruler. For that matter, the music of "Old Hundredth" is now widely viewed by many churchgoers as insufficiently cheerful. One can see what they mean, even if this criticism seems to forget that the joy and gladness of worshiping God might rightly be tinged with awe and a touch of fear. As for Beethoven's setting of Schiller's "Ode to Joy," no less a figure than Leo Tolstoy objected, for reasons I cannot comprehend, that this music is too elitist. Furthermore, almost everyone notices these days that when Schiller celebrates the Brotherhood of Man under the Fatherhood of God, he is taking masculinity to be the gender that is representative of both humanity and divinity.

Some of us may want, at points, to object to the objectors. We may believe that, at least in some cases, the integrity of the art and the poetry of the original text can better convey its life-transforming meaning than any amount of politically correct revision could do. But the issues of how to be more inclusive and more sensitive to injustice are serious, and often more serious than we find it convenient to acknowledge when we are in positions of privilege or power.

Let me illustrate my point with an example from a different art. In the year 2000, the Nobel Prize for Literature was awarded to the Chinese novelist and dramatist Gao Xingjian. This was the first time that the prize had been awarded to an author whose native language was Chinese. It is easy to imagine that this prestigious award could have been a cause for celebration in mainland China. But, as it happened, in China there was little or no news coverage given to the event. The reasons for this gap in coverage were two. First, Gao Xingjian's writings were little-known in China itself. And second, in Chinese literary circles where his work was indeed known, the general view was that he was writing works that appeal more to Westerners than to Chinese. Said one Chinese commentator: "The best Chinese novels and writers will never be accepted by Western audiences because [Westerners] evaluate them based on their own standards and values. Gao Xingjian is a perfect example. He was not accepted as a great novelist by either mainland or Taiwanese audiences." Another, sharper comment came from a thirty-year-old Chinese writer: "What a joke! I had never even heard of his name. This is a slap in the face to Chinese people. . . . Jin Yong [our best novelist] won't be accepted as a great writer by Western critics because he writes fantasy novels involving a strange mix of gods and humans."[10]

After the enormous worldwide popularity of the *Lord of the Rings* and of the Harry Potter novels, I am not so sure about the claim that fantasy fiction does not travel well outside Asia. But clearly the Nobel committee had blundered, despite the best of intentions. Because the committee was largely Western in make-up, it failed to guard against the possibility that it was unconsciously imposing standards of evaluation different from those used by the majority of Chinese. The act of extending the Nobel Prize to a Chinese author was received as an insult — the opposite of what was intended.

10. Quoted in *Persimmon: Asian Literature, Arts, and Culture* 2, no. 1 (Spring 2001): 38, 44-45.

If we do not recognize the dynamics of cultural exchange, we will forever blunder. And we may not even know it. In fact, a certain amount of blundering seems inevitable, no matter how hard we try. So it is essential that we examine our own motives and assumptions, paying attention to the specific context. And it is important to build up trust. When we trust the fundamental goodwill of one another, we do not magnify the mistakes that each other inevitably makes.

There are two very different activities that should not be confused. One is the activity of translating and transmitting our own songs so as to teach them to others. The other is translating and importing the songs of others so as to learn and enjoy them for ourselves. Of the two, the second activity, although not without its dangers, is less subject to abuse and misinterpretation. Imitation is a form of flattery, after all. And even "ripping off" the "good stuff" of other peoples is at least a kind of compliment, since it reflects some appreciation for what is taken. Whereas promoting one's own cultural products far and wide, especially when done from a position of greater power, can seem condescending or coercive.

The good news is that cultural exchange need not be viewed only with suspicion, as though it were always an act of co-opting or exploiting the other. I do not think that anyone is objecting when the North American composer John Adams incorporates Hispanic motifs and texts into his recent Nativity Oratorio called *El Niño*. Quite the contrary. Similarly, no passion oratorio in decades has received more acclaim, cross-culturally, than the *St. Mark Passion* composed in the year 2000 by Osvaldo Golijov. The son of an Orthodox Jewish mother and Russian atheist father, and raised in a Catholic environment in Argentina, Golijov says he approached this commission by asking himself, "How would Jesus live and act in Latin America? And how would Bach compose a Passion if he lived in South America at the end of the twentieth century?"[11] Golijov, in a characteristic move, incorporated African-influenced drum patterns into his music, because African

11. "Osvaldo Golijov and the *St. Mark Passion*," notes to the two-CD recording conducted by Maria Guinand, Haenssler Classic CD 98.404 (2000), p. 60.

slaves had been taken to Brazil and because he thought that the historical Jesus was more likely a person of color than a white person. Here one encounters a truly multicultural approach to religious music and song.

Influence goes back and forth in ways that, while sometimes anxiety-producing, can be exhilarating, creating a whole new sense of the world. One sees that in the German film *Nirgendwo in Afrika (Nowhere in Africa)*, which traces the story of Jewish refugees who fled from Germany to Kenya during Hitler's rise to power. Filmed in Kenya, it won the Academy Award for the Best Foreign Film in 2002. Most of us might find it difficult to say to what extent the score by Niki Reiser appropriately honors features of indigenous Kenyan music, but his music attempts to do so in its alternations and blendings of indigenous African and European-based styles.

Some of us with roots in the so-called West may not be aware of the extent to which the music of the West is often adopted elsewhere with great passion. It must be said that some of the finest contemporary recordings of Bach cantatas available anywhere in the world are from the Bach Collegium Japan, directed by Masaaki Suzuki. Moreover, as the enormous "sports star" popularity of the classical pianist Lang-Lang attests, the study of classical piano is all the rage in mainland China these days. And Western popular music is being consumed eagerly and adapted widely throughout South and East Asia. The mix itself can be invigorating. The popular British movie *Bend It Like Beckham* (USA release in 2003) tells the story of an Indian girl in Britain trying to break through all sorts of social and gender expectations in order to play football — what we in the United States call soccer. The musical soundtrack provides an intriguing and upbeat blend of Western popular music with popular music from South Asia. That same popular music from the Indian subcontinent shows mixed influences — including not only the Sufi Muslim Qawwali singing of the late Nusrat Fateh Ali Khan (which in his repetitions and improvisations often becomes rhapsodic in his praise of Sufi saints), but also Western pop rhythms and harmony. Returning to Christian song in particular, it is striking that, among today's Christians in China, nineteenth-century revival hymns such as "In the Sweet By and By" ("There's a Land That Is Fairer than Day") are still sung with as much dedication as when they were first brought to China by Western missionaries — complete with a concluding "Amen" that for Westerners recalls a bygone era in terms of singing practice.

Yet, even as we celebrate cross-cultural cross-pollination, we must register justifiable concerns that Western music is wiping out traditional musical styles that are ancient and often highly refined. Traditional Indian and Turkish music, for instance, uses many tones and intervals that are simply unavailable to instruments of Western origin, especially when tuned to Western scales. Under Western influence, such music is harder and harder to find. At the same time, ironically, music from other parts of the world (such as the Hindustani classical music of northern India) is being preserved by Westerners, in music schools in California and elsewhere. It is all very confusing. The lines of transmission and translation can become quite tangled!

Ecumenical Taste

When it comes to sharing our songs and deciding which songs to sing, are we stuck with power struggles and sheer relativism? Must we say that mere pragmatism rules, so that Christians and others should not bother about underlying standards and values? I have been suggesting that we should answer those questions with a resounding "No." In fact, I think we need to rule out at least two equally unacceptable alternatives. On the one hand, we do not want to try to claim, as many Christians used to, that we have access to a set of universal rules for good Christian music. We don't want Saint Francis dictating to all people, birds, and wolves exactly how they should sing praises to God! In that case, all of nature would probably be forever condemned to trying to sing Italian *laudi* in the manner of medieval traveling minstrels! But on the other hand, we cannot afford to shrug our shoulders and conclude that "anything goes." We should not be satisfied, any more than Francis would be, if birds and whales and people everywhere were to praise God carelessly, without any effort to offer God their best. I am being a little facetious, of course. But I think the point is clear.

There is a third way, a better way, which acknowledges the reality of standards but which sees that those musical standards emerge over time, and in particular communities. In this approach one pays attention to context. And one learns, gradually, to hear in the music of others more of what they themselves are hearing, and not to make judgments too quickly, either positively or negatively. Some kinds of music have a potentially wider audience than others. Some are more fitting than others for certain kinds of worship. But none of us can judge immediately what all kinds of music have to offer. And we need to learn to make judgments together (even in churches), given that expertise in one kind of music is no guarantee of expertise in another.

I conclude, therefore, with a proposal — rather modest but difficult enough: Let us commit ourselves to cultivating something we might call "ecumenical taste."[12] The word *ecumenical* comes, of course, from the Greek *oikoumene,* meaning the whole inhabited world. And normally we envision the world's "inhabitants" as human beings. But the canticle with which we began suggests that we need to expand what we mean by "inhabited" to include non-human inhabitants, as Saint Francis did in practice. Even more than Francis, however, we are in a position to be mindful of the ecological context of all creation and nature. In that way we relativize our divisions and remind ourselves of a pervasive (if hidden) interconnectedness of all things. But if one step toward ecumenical taste and awareness is expanding our sense of whom to think of as the world's community of inhabitants, a different step can be very local and intensely human. Our goal as it concerns worship in human communities is to encourage greater diversity and inclusion, combined with greater discernment and discipline. That is a task for individuals and for specific communities of Christians whose discipline and practice need to include sensitivity to art, music, and

---

12. See the chapter "Ecumenical Taste" in Brown, *Good Taste, Bad Taste, and Christian Taste,* pp. 160-98.

worship. Some of the biggest challenges of musical translation and transmission are not in crossing national or continental divides. They are in crossing the invisible lines between the choir loft (if any) and the pew, or between the so-called traditional service and contemporary service of the same congregation.

As will be evident, I am again returning to the theme with which I started when I was discussing the canticle composed by Saint Francis. But now it is with a different emphasis. In principle, all our praise and prayer ultimately includes the whole world as created and ordered for the glory of God. But in practice we sing and create and worship in one local setting. There, one way or another, we will face many of the challenges I've been describing. In doing so, we will have two aims, which exist in some tension with one another. The first aim, as I have said, is to become more inclusive and diverse, welcoming the songs of others (thereby honoring, in some sense, the songs of all creatures and creation), and sharing our songs in return. That is something especially pertinent to groups with greater levels of influence and power. The second aim is to become more discerning and disciplined. That will allow us to grow in faith, musically, and to develop our various kinds of music faithfully. Cultivating both of those capacities by the grace of God, we can realize more fully the power of communal song to provide us with a foretaste of the unending song and banquet to which God calls us.

CHAPTER 4

Is Good Art Good
for Christian Worship?

When Art Is Vital to Worship — or Not

A few years ago, the Princeton sociologist of religion Robert Wuthnow published a book-length study entitled *All in Sync: How Music and Art Are Revitalizing American Religion*. Basing his observations on interviews with approximately four hundred "ordinary people," Wuthnow argues in this book that the arts figure importantly in the "spiritual journeys" of most Americans — not only in their personal spirituality but also in American religious congregations. Although Wuthnow notes the relative superficiality of the spirituality fed by mass media, he contrasts such massively mediated and commercially propagated arts not only with the kinds of art found in museums and galleries but also with the communally based arts prominent in churches and synagogues.[1] Admitting that relatively few people in our time make a conscious link between religion and artistic creativity, Wuthnow nonetheless argues here, as he did earlier in a study of the spirituality of professional artists, that it is through artistic imagination, broadly conceived, that a great

---

1. Robert Wuthnow, *All in Sync: How Music and Art Are Revitalizing American Religion* (Berkeley: University of California Press, 2003), p. xiv.

many of those who practice religion are discovering a vital sort of faith today.[2]

In *All in Sync,* Wuthnow takes an admirably non-elitist view of the artistic processes and products that seem to be spiritually renewing; he concludes, for instance, with a chapter entitled "The Artist in Everyone." But in being so relatively egalitarian — which is the only way he could claim to be describing a broad swath of American religious culture — Wuthnow gives us cause to wonder. Would the kinds of art that he says are revitalizing American religion be regarded as creative or exceptionally good by most people trained in the respective arts? When Wuthnow asserts, for instance, that the quality of music in church matters to congregations, he supports that claim by noting how people prefer that the singing in church not be "off key," and he points out that congregations often like "familiar tunes or hymns that are simple enough to remember."[3] That is certainly not much to ask, when it comes to music. The standards of musical quality that Wuthnow cites regarding church music are plainly those of the average worshiper, not the criteria of composers, organists, and choir directors, many of whom are known to gravitate toward more complex or subtle forms of worship music.

One could argue that, even at their best, the kinds of art attracting the attention of spiritual seekers and worshipers these days are more frequently on the order of the "Left Behind" novels by Tim LaHaye and Jerry Jenkins or *The Da Vinci Code* by Dan Brown than they are on the level of Marilynne Robinson's novel *Gilead* or Toni Morrison's *Beloved.* Musically speaking, the popular "classic" praise chorus "Our God Is an Awesome God" (albeit without all the attendant verses) seems more representative of the music of the devout than the *St. Mark Passion* by Osvaldo Golijov, popular as that new work has been in certain circles. If we are to believe Wuthnow's evidence, if not his exact words, the works and styles that highly trained artists and critics typi-

2. See Robert Wuthnow, *Creative Spirituality: The Way of the Artist* (Berkeley and Los Angeles: University of California Press, 2001).

3. Wuthnow, *Creative Spirituality,* p. 180.

cally regard as representative of artistry at its best are not generally the ones that are most influential in revitalizing American religion.

The potential religious charisma of low-status art is by no means an exclusively American phenomenon, of course. And it is not a *new* phenomenon, in many respects. In ancient Athens, it seems, the statue of Athena that remained most popular in religious practice even into the classical period was not the large, beautifully wrought ivory-and-gold statue from the hand of the famous sculptor Phidias, which was installed within the Parthenon. Rather, the sculpture regarded as more sacred by the people in general was apparently a much smaller, cruder olive-wood statue originating in the rituals of antiquity, which was housed in the Erechtheion Temple on the Acropolis.[4]

There is something about this that might well give us pause. Ever since the Romantic era (and before), thinkers have been struck by analogies, at least, between art and religion, and by the way in which great art can be inspirational. Although the Romantics fostered democratic ideals too, and admired the craft of humble artisans, Romanticism became associated even more with the cult of Art with a capital "A," and of the artistic genius. When modern religious thought has attended to the arts, it has often reflected that kind of elevated — not to mention inflated — view of art and artists.

What is different about the present beginning point is that I am suggesting it would be unwise not to take account of religious art, particularly art in worship, that is by no means great and that may even lack what the Romantics saw as the integrity of a humble craft.[5] And I do

---

4. See Jon D. Mikalson, *Athenian Popular Religion,* reprint ed. (Chapel Hill: University of North Carolina Press, 1987).

5. Lately, many studies of art and music from a religious standpoint have examined popular and material culture without privileging the high arts, and in some cases have consciously given priority to popular media and music. See, for example, David Morgan, *Visual Piety: A History and Theory of Popular Religious Images* (Berkeley and Los Angeles: University of California Press, 1998); Colleen McDannell, *Material Christianity: Religion and Popular Culture in America* (New Haven, Conn.: Yale University Press, 1995); Tex Sample, *Powerful Persuasion: Multimedia Witness in Christian Worship* (Nashville: Abingdon Press, 2005); and an earlier book by Sample, *White Soul: Country Music, the Church, and Working Americans* (Nashville: Abingdon Press, 1996).

so without forgetting worries about artistic quality and integrity in media with mass appeal. Modern technology as exploited by the immensely profitable entertainment industry, for example, has put many artisan crafts out of business even as it has made possible the marketing of a kind of commercial artistic "product" that is in many respects (as has often been observed) the artistic equivalent of fast food. The instant and widespread appeal of much commercial art and music is undeniable but too often seductive. Whereas fast food of dubious nutritional value plays on the human weakness for the quick pleasures of sugar, salt, and fat (and easy access), the corresponding appeal of commercial art is that it too is easy to take in because it is formulaic and typically plays on the human weakness for such things as flashy special effects, superficial erotic stimulation, sentimental story lines, or violent visual and audible excitement.

Having noted that, we should also keep in mind that popular religious art of the sort scorned by the art world, whether considered relatively crude and simplistic or outrageously cheap and "cheesy," is of course rarely felt to be inferior or religiously expendable by those many people whose spirituality relies on such artistic means. And, as I have already noted, not everything scorned by artistic elites is really just "fast food," aesthetically speaking. Or if it is, it may at times resemble such comparatively nutritious items as the grilled Asian chicken salad, or even organic vegetarian side dishes, now appearing at fast-food chains worldwide.

In any case, the available evidence suggests that not only can Christian worship survive dubious art; it can also sometimes make good use of such art — art that by the standards of the art world would be judged mediocre or bad: what artists and critics call kitsch, for example.[6] There is no direct correspondence, overall, between artistic merit and religious value. On the contrary, it seems plain that good worship (sincere prayer and uplifting praise, for instance) thrives at times by means of art that isn't very good — admitting that

---

6. See Frank Burch Brown, *Good Taste, Bad Taste, and Christian Taste* (New York: Oxford University Press, 2000), pp. 128-59.

there will always be differences of opinion about which art should count as good.

An essay on the role (if any) of good art in worship and the Christian life is not the place to try to imagine all the reasons why inferior art or art with low artistic status might be good for religion, at least under certain circumstances. It may be enough in this context to recall that, in a worship setting, art is seldom used or experienced in isolation from other practices such as Scripture reading, preaching, and corporate prayer. In that larger context, art that might seem trivial or weak in some respects can nonetheless make a contribution. And possible artistic deficiencies can turn into relative strengths. Many a congregational song that might sound sentimental to discriminating musical ears can be redeemed, as it were, by the larger purposes of singing together in worship and by the fact that the melody is easily remembered and widely enjoyed, whatever trained musicians might think of it.

The extensive and apparently legitimate Christian use of questionable art gives us all the more reason to wonder whether and how *good* art could ever be good for worship — and whether the features that make something good as art are to some extent also those that make it good liturgically. As we will soon see, in pursuing such questions we need to go beyond our everyday ways of sorting out the good from the bad in both art and worship. In the meantime, painful as the process may be for artists and religious lovers of art, we need to look more closely at some of the more cogent (if not entirely persuasive) reasons that have been given for how and why good art may *not* always be good for religion in general, let alone for worship in particular.

Religious Doubts about Good Art

In his influential book *The Analogical Imagination* (1981), the Catholic theologian David Tracy asks whether the qualities that make something exceptionally good artistically are likely to make it exceptionally good religiously. And he denies that this is so. Admitting that in rare instances an artistic classic can at the same time be a religious classic, Tracy insists that this is indeed exceptional — which helps explain why, in Tracy's long discussion of the idea of the religious classic, he mostly treats classics of art as belonging to a genre that is different from the religious classic, although analogous. His argument, in a nutshell, is that religion has as its core subject and source something too encompassing, boundless, and self-shattering to be expressed or contained in art — the heart of religion being something Tracy describes rather enigmatically as "a manifestation of the whole by the power of that whole, not ourselves."[7] According to Tracy, such a radically disruptive manifestation of "incomprehensible mystery" is inconsistent with what he characterizes as "the sureness of form of the major artistic classics."[8] This is not to deny that sometimes in the very greatest classics of art the "triumph of form" can miraculously occur partly by working in and through what at one level are formal flaws. Most artistic classics are not of that sort, Tracy says.

Tracy acknowledges exceptional cases in which artistic classics are also religious ones. He names, for instance, the Psalms, the prose of Augustine and Kierkegaard, the poetry of Dante and Milton — but no music (as far as I can tell), or architecture such as the Chartres Cathedral or the Ronchamp Chapel of Le Corbusier, and few paintings on the order of Masaccio's *Trinity* (1427; Sta. Maria Novella, Florence). Tracy asserts that even the rare artistic religious classics are not, "under the same rules of production, identically both [artistic and religious] at the same time."[9] In other words, the artistic goals are necessarily different in kind from the religious goals. Perhaps Tracy could find a place for a musical art of the sublime, such as one hears in the *Livre du Saint Sacrement* of Olivier Messiaen (1908-92) or, still more recently, in many compositions of the Finnish composer Einojuhani Rautavaara (b. 1928), which create a whirl of sonic mist that draws us toward the infinite. Tracy might also approve of the minimalist tech-

7. David Tracy, *The Analogical Imagination: Christian Theology and the Culture of Pluralism* (New York: Crossroad, 1981), p. 197. For a related but rather different and much earlier discussion of Tracy's views of the matter, see my book *Religious Aesthetics* (Princeton, N.J.: Princeton University Press, 1989), pp. 161-65.

8. Tracy, *The Analogical Imagination*, p. 200, p. 197.

9. Tracy, *The Analogical Imagination*, p. 201.

niques of the contemporary Estonian composer Arvo Pärt (b. 1935), which evoke the contemplative, Hesychast tradition of Eastern Christianity. He would presumably grant, as well, the religious value of seventeenth-century Protestant poems that Stanley Fish and others have identified as self-consuming artifacts, devoutly emptying their artistry of any claim to self-sufficiency. But most of the best art — really *classic* art — Tracy says, is too preoccupied with striving for its own aesthetic perfection to serve as a fundamental religious reference point or as a normative religious expression.

Certainly on that point Tracy would have gotten no argument from Søren Kierkegaard, whose worries about aestheticism we considered briefly in the very first chapter. In his book of 1850 entitled *Practice in Christianity,* Kierkegaard writes that, just as it is incomprehensible to him how a murderer can calmly sharpen the knife with which he will commit his crime, so is it incomprehensible to him how an artist can sit "year in and year out occupied in the work of painting Christ — without having it occur to him whether Christ would wish to be painted, would wish to have his portrait . . . depicted by [the artist's] master brush." Kierkegaard believes that the artist should give up, and not because the artist has been painting so badly but because the artist has been painting so well. Inviting us to imagine the situation of a superb artist who has painted a Crucifixion, Kierkegaard finds it entirely plausible that what people will admire is the artistic expertise for its own sake. They will look for "whether the play of colors is right, and the shadows, whether blood looks like that, whether the suffering expression is artistically true." Kierkegaard declares that what was once the "actual suffering of the Holy One, the artist has somehow turned into money and admiration."[10] Attracted by an art of such polish and accomplishment, lovers of art miss the religious point. They fail to realize that "Christ has required only imitators" — that is, people who would actually follow him and pattern their lives on his.[11]

10. Søren Kierkegaard, *Practice in Christianity,* ed. and trans. Howard V. Hong and Edna H. Hong (Princeton, N.J.: Princeton University Press, 1991), p. 255.

11. For more on Kierkegaard's point and the opposition to that point, see Brown, *Good Taste, Bad Taste, and Christian Taste,* pp. 30-32.

One could fairly but prematurely conclude from all this that the primary practical theological question about art should not be how to make art that is good enough to serve religious ends — since (on this view) the better the art, qua art, the worse its religious effect is likely to be. Rather, the question should seemingly be whether, from a religious perspective, it would be better to have overtly unassuming and imperfect art or *no art at all*. Some Christians have opted for a healthy tolerance of bad art, cheap art — even what has come to be termed kitsch — so that grace may abound. Tracy, albeit without giving thanks for kitsch, evidently welcomes art that falls short of classic status aesthetically, so that it might just possibly give rise to a kind of non-aesthetic truth-event that could disclose a reality infinitely greater than the art or self of the maker. For his part, Kierkegaard knows that a truly good artist, when painting a Crucifixion scene, will not settle for painting it badly. But he thinks that painting it well is likely to be a religious distraction, sidetracking the artist from true devotion and distracting the viewer into purely aesthetic appreciation. Hence, his advice in the writing quoted earlier is that the artist should give up the attempt to serve religion artistically. Even in terms of literary art, Kierkegaard is never quite able to conceive of how his being what he terms "a kind of poet" could actually make a vital contribution to discipleship itself.

Now, it is rare for religious leaders and thinkers to go to quite such extremes in questioning the religious value of good art. And it is hard to imagine what some of this advice would look like in practice. While most of us can enjoy religious art that falls far short of greatness, would we really want to object that John Donne's metaphysical poetry aims too high, both artistically and religiously? Would Michael Crosbie want to abandon the range of aesthetic and religious ideals evident in his two books on *Architecture for the Gods*[12] and urge us, instead, to gaze upon Samuel Butcher's Precious Moments Chapel in Carthage, Missouri, which is certainly kitsch, whatever else it may be?

As for music, didn't Luther (or, more probably, someone later put-

12. Michael J. Crosbie, *Architecture for the Gods,* vol. 1 (Mulgrave, Victoria: Images, 1999); and *Architecture for the Gods,* vol. 2 (Mulgrave, Victoria: Images, 2002).

ting words in his mouth) want to make sure the devil did not get to have all the good, beautiful melodies? Did he not have harsh words for those who could not appreciate the "amazing" art of polyphony shown in works of high musical artistry that would allow one "to taste with wonder (yet not to comprehend) God's absolute and perfect wisdom"?[13] Isn't there a point to the long tradition of calling J. S. Bach the "Fifth Evangelist"? Again, didn't John Wesley have good reason to argue that the hymns of his brother Charles were an artistically worthy exercise in practical divinity, with genuine poetic merit?[14] And wasn't "The Constitution on the Sacred Liturgy," from Vatican II, right to praise the beauty of human arts as glorifying God — and to insist, also, that the treasury of sacred music is to be preserved and cultivated with great care?[15]

The questions mount. How can we square the intuitions most of us still have about the religious value of good art with the doubts we've seen expressed regarding the role of good art in serving God and the church? What explains the dissonance between the desire to extol the religious value of good art and the unabated — indeed, zealous — religious use of artistically inferior works, together with a recurrent theological impulse to deprecate genuine artistic goodness as inappropriate or beside the point religiously?

I have set forth various religious objections to good art not because I think they are trivial but because I think they are significant, even if one-sided. If we want to advocate the religious vocation of various kinds of good art, whether in its classic forms or in some other guise,

13. Martin Luther, Foreword to Georg Rhau's *Symphoniae jucundae* of 1538, quoted in Friedrich Blume et al., *Protestant Church Music* (London: Victor Gollancz, 1975), p. 9. The ever-outspoken Luther went so far as to say that people unaffected by such wondrous music "deserve to hear a certain filthy poet or the music of the pigs" (p. 9).

14. John Wesley, Preface to *A Collection of Hymns for the Use of the People Called Methodists* (1780), vol. 7 in the *Works of John Wesley*, 26 vols., ed. Franz Hildebrandt and Oliver A. Beckerlegge (Oxford: Oxford University Press/Clarendon, 1983), p. 74.

15. "The Constitution on the Sacred Liturgy," in *Vatican Council II: Constitutions, Decrees, Declarations*, revised translation in inclusive language, ed. Austin Flannery (Northport, N.Y.: Costello, 1996), pp. 117-61. See Chapter VI, "Sacred Music," pp. 152-55.

then it is imperative to take into account the doubters. Accordingly, as I prepare to frame something of a theological apologia for good art, I want to rephrase the objections already considered, contextualizing them in terms of concepts and themes commonly encountered at a more popular level.

Toward a Religious Defense of Good Art

Today religious suspicions regarding rigorously disciplined and culti-vated arts — whether in North America, Europe, India, or elsewhere — surface in variants of the arguments we have already considered. These variants come down to three common, related criteria for reli-giously worthy art: first, simplicity; second, expressive or emotional power; and third, popular appeal. Satisfying the first two criteria, which tend to be linked, results in relatively simple and emotive art that is likely to be popular (thus meeting the third criterion). The crite-rion of popularity, however, often functions in near isolation. In fact, the perception that a given style of music is likeable or appealing (pop-ular) is increasingly regarded as sufficient to consider the art in ques-tion "good enough" for church use, and appropriate for worship, at least as long as religious words are attached and a religious purpose is clearly intended.[16] Thus many songs originally performed by pop solo-ists or small bands, using a syncopated style that is hard for most North American congregations to sing, are nonetheless accepted by many congregations because of the music's contemporary feel and popular appeal.

Yet even the criterion of popularity can quickly be watered down or seemingly abandoned, as we can see in Rick Warren's approach in his best-selling book *The Purpose Driven Life*. In that book Warren writes, in the spirit of outreach, "Worship has nothing to do with the

---

16. See William Easum, *Dancing with Dinosaurs: Ministry in a Hostile and Hurting World* (Nashville: Abingdon Press, 1993). For an extended critique of such views, see Brown, *Good Taste, Bad Taste, and Christian Taste*, pp. 233-51.

style or volume or speed of a song. God loves all kinds of music because he invented it all — fast and slow, loud and soft, old and new. You probably don't like it all, but God does! If it is offered to God in spirit and truth, it is an act of worship."[17] While laudably hospitable and inviting, such an approach misses something important. Although this assertion offers a welcome gesture toward becoming more inclusive, it provides no practical criteria for discerning quality or appropriateness beyond the spirit in which the music is offered — something only God can really know for sure. The direct implication is that it would be un-Christian not to accept every kind of music in worship, just as God accepts every kind of person who responds to the gospel. But when one recalls that "worship" in this sense is something public and communal, not merely private devotion, one has every reason to ask if Warren would make the same statement about sermons. Would any conscientious congregation embrace the idea that God loves all sincere sermons, regardless of how they are delivered or whether they are scripturally sound? Similarly, we might well ask whether it makes good sense to say that God "invented" every imaginable kind of preaching. Clearly not. Just as, in practice, no church accepts all sermons as edifying and God-given, no church can or should embrace all music without considering quality or theological soundness or suitability for worship.

In any case, people who ask that all kinds of music be welcome in church rarely mean what they say. Today many such calls to be musically all-inclusive have the hidden (or not so hidden) agenda of promoting popular music that traditional proponents of so-called good church music have normally resisted as unworthy. The criterion of popularity thus sneaks in by the back door.

On top of the negative judgments of David Tracy and Søren Kierkegaard concerning the religious liabilities of exceptionally good art, therefore, we need to add the populist Christian objection that it is

17. Rick Warren, *The Purpose Driven Life* (Grand Rapids: Zondervan, 2002), p. 65. For a discussion of Warren's comments that places them in the context of a practical theology of worship music, see also Chapter 6 in this volume, "Religious Music and Secular Music: A Calvinist Perspective, Re-formed."

wrong to introduce questions of artistic quality into a Christian setting, when those questions lead to rejecting many people's favorite
styles of music and art. This often ends up ruling out many classic
forms of "good art." As some have put it, ostensibly good art and music that fail to connect with the majority of everyday worshipers are
out of sync with the times ("culturally irrelevant"), probably elitist,
and in many instances representative of class privilege and power. It is
thus bad for evangelism, useless for church growth, and probably
downright un-Christian.[18]

By now we have assembled a long list of reasons for taking what
most musicians and educators in the arts have traditionally seen as the
best art and removing it from the list of what is religiously desirable.
Without denying that there is considerable validity to some of the
charges we have gleaned and laid out, I will be arguing from this point
on that the resulting composite image of the religious hazards of good
art is distorted from both an aesthetic and a theological point of view.

Let us consider first the suspicions voiced by David Tracy in his discussion of religious classics. When Tracy denies that these classics are
well suited to functioning, at the same time, as religious classics, his argument seems most plausible when we recall that — as others have
pointed out repeatedly — the standards of the Western institutions of
high art, with their emphasis on individual expression, originality, and
autonomy, do not coincide with customary religious expectations for
art. Until recently, those modern institutions of high art have in fact
tended to marginalize what is religious. They have done so in their
very conception of art as essentially autonomous, requiring a narrowly
aesthetic attention to formal traits and to intrinsically expressive qualities. And they have done so in practice, since it has been common, until recently, to treat the specifically religious features of art and music
as artistically and aesthetically irrelevant when performing or displaying works that originally served religious functions.

It has gradually dawned on many of us, however, that much of the
potential artistic interest of those works (altarpieces, devotional paint-

18. See Easum, *Dancing with Dinosaurs*, pp. 85-89.

ings, and works of religious music, for example) dissipates when the larger religious and cultural connections are treated as irrelevant, since the art forms themselves are shaped to a purpose beyond merely aesthetic contemplation in the narrow sense. And the narrowly aesthetic notion of art is inadequate even when dealing with much modern artistry. If one listens to Benjamin Britten's *War Requiem* for the "music alone," ignoring the way the work as music attempts to reckon morally and religiously with the effects of war, one misses most of what has made this musical work a modern classic. Again, one might consider what is most musically involving about John Adams's 9/11 memorial orchestral work *On the Transmigration of Souls,* which was premiered by the New York Philharmonic and which won the 2003 Pulitzer prize in music. What draws the listener most acutely has everything to do with the experience of loss and remembrance and little to do with "purely musical" abstract patterns of sounds (although one can take an interest in those, too).

Equally good examples can be found in architecture, both Christian and non-Christian. Chartres Cathedral and the Hagia Sophia in Istanbul are surely classics of both art and religion. And the reasons they are religious classics are integrally related to the reasons they are deemed classic in artistic and aesthetic terms. It is not as though the architectural combination of mystery with a rational formal order and beautiful symbolism is irrelevant to either the religious goals or the aesthetic aims of these works.[19] Something similar can be said of many Hindu temples of South India, whether in Chennai or Kanchipurum or Mudrai or Chidambaram. Their outer and inner forms reflect harmonious mathematical proportions that generate (for some Christians as well as many Hindus) a religious sense of joy and peace, while their exterior niches accommodate thousands of sculptures exuding infinite abundance, playfulness, and awe-inspiring grandeur that most Hindus see as derived from the ultimately one divine reality. Within their

19. For one classic study of this very principle in Gothic architecture, see Otto von Simson, *The Gothic Cathedral: Origins of Gothic Architecture and the Medieval Concept of Order,* 3rd ed. (Princeton, N.J.: Princeton University Press, 1988).

gates, such temples incorporate multiple corridors for clockwise pilgrimage toward their central shrines, all the while providing a proliferation of foci befitting Hindu spirituality.[20] Everything about the architectural plan is ordered to purposes that are at once aesthetically involving and religiously transformative, assuming one is attuned to that mode of spirituality and that sometimes overwhelming mode of temple design. The artistry of these temples has thus become for many a primary expression of a way of being religious, and vice versa.

As for a possible residual suspicion that (as Tracy's argument would claim) a classic or great work of art is bound to be too self-assured in form to serve religious purposes, we can admit that a pursuit of formal excellence is not necessarily religious. But it is by no means obvious why an artwork's formal achievement would necessarily undermine or distract from its religious aspirations, any more than a well-wrought form would necessarily undermine a book of theology or a sermon. We should not confuse formal discipline and a pursuit of well-wrought and rewarding design with pride and spiritual complacency, either in theology or in art.

The question we need to pose to Tracy, then, is whether we should allow those Western high-art traditions to control our idea of what should count as an artistic classic, or indeed as genuinely and intrinsically artistic. If we are attentive in our theories to the kinds of engagement that much art invites, whether that artistry be great or merely good, I believe we have reason to understand art and aesthetics rather differently.

According to the aesthetic theory I am putting forward (here and elsewhere), art and religion are at times integrally related even while retaining considerable autonomy. There are different genres of art with their own sets of criteria, some of which are shaped by religious and moral purposes that must be taken into account in judging the art to be a good work of its kind. Such adjustments in criteria, from genre to genre, are nothing strange to art. Many a song text that seems lame

20. See, for example, George Michell, *The Hindu Temple: An Introduction to Its Meaning and Forms* (New York: Harper & Row/Icon Editions, 1977).

or else inflated, when read on its own as poetry, makes for a beautiful libretto or lyric when set to music. To judge an artwork's quality in relation to its genre and purpose is not to abandon artistic criteria but to adjust them. This assumes that, in the process of evaluating the excellence of something as art, one could be concerned, finally, not only with what is unique to art simply as art but also with what allows artistry to play a unique and integral role in religion or morality, and vice versa. What is unique and artistically engaging about the plays of Shakespeare and Aeschylus, or the architecture of the Parthenon and the Pantheon, or indeed the art of the greatest filmmakers, may have less to do with what of life they exclude than with how they incorporate and transform life commitments, values, and beliefs in the process of pursuing their artistic goals. But if that is the case, it follows that the goals and goods of art may sometimes and in some ways coincide with the goals and goods of religion — goals (such as a transformation of vision and commitment) that religion itself cannot attain in the same way without such art.[21]

To suppose, as Tracy appears to do, that the goals and principles intrinsic to the best art are almost inevitably distinct from the goals of religion may also imply something misleading about religion itself — namely, that it is somehow incidental that religion in its peak moments so often seeks out the poetic, the musical, the dramatic. But isn't that notion highly improbable, whatever Kierkegaard sometimes said? As Kierkegaard would have insisted, religion at its highest is concerned with the transformation of one's whole being and commitment in relation to God, others, and the world. If something like this can be said of the higher goals of religious life, it seems clear that those goals might at times not only accommodate but also positively require some sort of artistry. For artistry is distinctive in being able to engage one's whole being. It can provide sensory and imaginative embodiment of larger visions and commitments — larger and more vivid than we can clearly

21. For two representative critiques of "high modernist" and purist aesthetics from a religious or Christian perspective, see Nicholas Wolterstorff, *Art in Action: Toward a Christian Aesthetic* (Grand Rapids: William B. Eerdmans, 1980); and Brown, *Religious Aesthetics.*

conceive or plainly say — and in that way move the will, the mind, the emotions, and the spirit.

It is true that much religion that takes an ascetic or prophetic course curbs the sensory and the aesthetic. But scriptural prophecy itself often requires a kind of imagination and poetic rhetoric, whether that is conceived of as divine or as human in origin. And even ascetic rituals have their own aesthetic, as in the beautifully spare interiors of medieval Cistercian monasteries and the austere beauties of chant.

We can concede Kierkegaard's point that when a religious artwork is also an artistic classic, it can be appreciated to a large extent without giving assent to its religious symbols and without taking much interest in its religious aims as such. Many listeners enjoy the musical artistry of Bach's *Mass in B Minor* and his *Passion According to St. Matthew* by listening to them simply as concert works and perhaps without having any sense of the words. But that is not the same as saying that the primary artistic goals at the core of this music by Bach do not fundamentally coincide with his evident religious aim of interpreting musically the main themes, affirmations, and stories of Christian faith. The same can be said of the greatest hymns, both music and text. The strengths of such music are at once religious and aesthetic: imaginative depth, emotional engagement, a sense of transcendence beyond the merely mundane, and the transformation of a sense of sin, loss, and death into an exalted vision of inner and outer joy and peace. Religious listeners may be the ones most likely to hear all this as integral to the music. But it is always the case that some members of an audience are better positioned than others to grasp certain relevant features of a work of art.

But how might engagement with such artistry become a part of discipleship, a religious and Christian discipline? Not all religious listeners will be prepared to grasp the salient features of the *Mass in B Minor* — and in some cases that could be because those listeners are accustomed to turning to art only for light entertainment, or to religion only for simple assurance and comfort. Such music asks something different. Thus, when Bach, in his setting of the Creed, first comes to the text *"et exspecto resurrectionem mortuorum,"* he does not move immediately to an outright affirmation of the expectation of the resurrection of the dead, as though that were an indubitable and perfectly straightforward matter. Instead, he draws the listener through mystifying harmonic shifts filled with dissonance and tension, which very much deepen the sense of mystery involved in the affirmation of resurrection. This is no glib faith being affirmed musically, but a faith being led to confront the unspeakable and imponderable, which issues ultimately in "inexpressible" joy, an astonishing dance of resurrection, exulting to the pulse of divine delight in and through all things. Perhaps Bach had in mind 1 Corinthians 15:51-52, which Handel sets to music in *Messiah:* "Behold, I tell you a mystery: We shall not all sleep; but we shall all be changed . . . at the last trumpet."

At some point, of course, art alone is insufficient, even at its highest. So is theology, however, or preaching or ritual. Speaking in terms familiar to many religions, nothing we know as humans is completely fulfilling or beatific, apart from grace and the primordial source and goal that is more than anything we can create ourselves. Even the highest art cannot coerce a fitting response, but can only involve and invite.

That said, I would nonetheless reaffirm that much art at its highest (whether or not its subject is explicitly religious) joins religion at its highest, and becomes integral to that. That can happen in two contrasting ways. There is a kind of self-emptying of art in which the medium is effaced and reduced to virtually nothing, as it were, so that silence or near-silence prevails. One thinks of the spiritual minimalism of contemporary music by Arvo Pärt or John Tavener, or certain kinds of chant. Even in that "negative" tradition, however, the process of paring away often has an integral shape and rhythm that is at least minimally aesthetic and requires artful attention. As for when religion takes the opposite direction by expressing faith and truth at their fullest and most persuasive, that can rarely happen through a medium utterly devoid of aesthetic shape and imagination.

The late philosopher and fiction writer Iris Murdoch writes memorably and believably when, in her dialogue *Acastos,* she has her fictive Socrates declare (somewhat atypically),

We are mixed beings, . . . mixed of darkness and light, sense and intellect, flesh and spirit — the language of art is the highest native natural language of that condition. . . . We are all artists, we are all storytellers. We all have to live by art, it's our daily bread. . . . And we should thank the gods for great artists who draw away the veil of anxiety and selfishness and show us, even for a moment, another world . . . and tell us a little bit of truth.[22]

Perhaps, despite acknowledging the inevitable imperfections of everything human, this passage retains a little too much of the Romantic idealization of art. Murdoch steps onto shaky ground when she has her Socrates embrace the idea that "good art tells us more truth about our lives and our world than any other kind of thinking or speculation."[23] That encomium to art is insufficiently dialectical — as though art could "tell" such truth all by itself. But Murdoch is rightly referring to specific kinds of truth: the truths that matter to our "mixed" creaturely existence as spiritually embodied beings. If this high understanding of the potential of art (including the narrative and poetry of Scripture) is even remotely plausible, it suggests how inadequate the use of art must be when religion is tempted simply to employ artistic effects in order to create a popular appeal, or to provide spiritual warm-up exercises. To reduce art to a utilitarian role dictated solely in terms of doctrine or pre-fabricated ritual is to do an injustice both to art and to worship, as Pope Benedict XVI has argued in writings discussed in a later chapter.

But to say even that is not to say enough, if by "worship" we are thinking only of the conventional forms of liturgy and common prayer. After all, the Christian life in all its dimensions is to be, in the largest sense, an act of worship and prayer. We need to acknowledge, therefore, a potentially central role for aesthetic and artistic imagination within religious life as a whole, and within the Christian life specifically, and that is true most of all because Christianity

22. Iris Murdoch, *Acastos: Two Platonic Dialogues* (New York: Penguin Books, 1986), pp. 62, 63.
23. Murdoch, *Acastos*, p. 63.

finally calls for a kind of total conversion in which faithful assent and what we call aesthetic imagination interact, combine, and are changed together.

Concluding Considerations

There are some issues that remain for consideration and clarification. For one thing, someone might still want to object that many works of art cannot be classic for religious practice simply because of their limited audience. However, one could make that same argument against a number of acknowledged theological classics that are seldom read by anyone but a highly educated and theologically devoted minority. There is also the question of the limitations of time and space of public worship as commonly practiced. Those necessarily rule out many of the more developed and expansive kinds of art, which play a worshipful role, therefore, mostly outside the context of worship services as normally practiced. Perhaps, however — as many are discovering — it is time to take more seriously the possibility that worship can rightly take the shape of sacred concerts, for instance, or of paraliturgical services in which art (drama, music, video) plays a much greater role.

None of this simply conflates art and religion, or re-instates certain Romantic notions of high art as, in effect, a substitute for religion. Nor does it imply that the work of art must be great in itself in order to be good both artistically and religiously. Many religious rituals, major and minor, are rich in dramatic qualities without needing to be considered "dramas" in the fullest sense, let alone great art. And, as we had reason to note earlier, there are many rewarding artistic products that, without being major achievements as individual works of art, are indeed major forces in the sphere of religion. The Virgin of Guadalupe as seen in popular images is surely a religious classic among Hispanic Christians in the New World, and possibly beyond, even if few specific renditions of the image are likely to be considered remarkable as works of art per se. Alejandro

García-Rivera, among others, has demonstrated their importance quite convincingly.[24]

This observation, while perhaps easy to accept in principle, has far-reaching implications. It means, for instance, that any adequate study of Hispanic spirituality and worship in the New World would probably need to take that image into account. (The same could be said of the need for studies of Protestantism to take hymnody seriously.) The fact that many theologies and histories of Christianity ignore such images just indicates that most scholars have not been trained to recognize the crucial religious role of those kinds of works and to give an account of the difference they make in religious faith and practice.

This leads us naturally to the significant question of whose artworks one is regarding as good, religiously, and whether there aren't many good works of local or regional religious artistry that make no claim to having a universal appeal. This is part of a larger question that is familiar in cultural criticism by now — the question of whose perceptions count in evaluating what is good, whether in art or in religion.

Ironically, it is perhaps the failure to recognize the power and artistry of many forms of popular religious art that has contributed most to the still widespread theological neglect of the arts. As long as art of high quality is presumed to be the special province of the privileged, and as long as popular art is seen, at the same time, as inevitably derivative and illustrative, or as merely entertaining, theologians and religious historians are likely to leave art of both kinds to the specialists.

Thus, to the earlier charge that the religious advocacy of good art is invariably linked with some of kind of elitism, we can now reply that nothing combats elitism better than the recognition of good art in multiple kinds and in many spheres. The elitist typically believes that the standards of good art are in the possession of a special group attuned to the best art (typically identified with interests of the socially influential and/or highly educated). That assumption is untenable, however,

24. Alejandro García-Rivera, *The Community of the Beautiful: A Theological Aesthetics* (Collegeville, Minn.: Liturgical Press/Michael Glazier, 1999), pp. 192-96.

because taste is culturally conditioned, even if not culturally confined; and no one group, regardless of training and aesthetic capacity, is positioned to detect and judge the qualities of all forms of artistic goodness regardless of the style or medium.

Here, however, we must emphasize that to attend to the contextual factors involved in good art is by no means to surrender or totally relativize all standards of artistic quality in the name of religious hospitality and inclusiveness. Those who treat religious kitsch as spiritually harmless, for example, may be right in some contexts; sometimes kitsch may even be religiously good, as a quick and easy way of freeing up appropriate emotions that might otherwise remain inaccessible or frozen. But kitsch — because it plays on easy emotions and reflexive responses — is forever immature. Religious expression is eventually cheapened when it is tied extensively to art forms or subgenres that are widely recognized by those involved in the respective arts as superficial and possibly exploitive.

Once one acknowledges the multiplicity of good kinds of art, one can see that it is important not to try to force inappropriate criteria and expectations on a particular kind of art. For one thing, not all art that is good should be seen or promoted as "universal." Mahler's symphonies, Wagner's operas, John Coltrane's jazz improvisations, and Hindustani classical music from India all elicit negative responses from many astute listeners outside their orbit. And yet it makes little sense to deny, on that account, that such music is of a high order artistically. Similarly, gospel music even at its best does not fit every worship setting, nor does it strike all astute listeners as music worth promoting. But that says more about the cultural and contextual factors involved in music perception than it does about whether there is good gospel music.

It is equally important to recognize that not all good art and music needs to be regarded as somehow beautiful. Much art — the genre of the blues, for example — is conceived, rather, in terms of authentic expression, which in the case of the blues may be soulful and earthy in a way that resists being heard as merely beautiful. Much modern and contemporary art of moral and spiritual significance is baffling, grotesque, and even shocking, defying ready classification among the world's beauties. There are those who still may want to expand the use of the words *beauty* and *beautiful* to cover the whole wide array of excellent artistry — from Gregorian chant to grunge rock, and from Renaissance Madonnas to the often intentionally frightening masks used in traditional ritual ceremonies in many parts of the world. But it is not clear what that accomplishes, especially if it risks importing Enlightenment, medieval, or Platonic notions of beauty that might be quite misleading. While the recent recovery of the concept of beauty in theological and critical circles is to be applauded, such a concept must be handled carefully if it is not to obscure more than it enlightens. The promotion of beauty at all costs could easily lead to the religious neglect of art that needs to be difficult and perhaps in some ways disquieting or disgusting in order to achieve its proper religious ends.[25] The agitated or possibly alarming sounds in Christian heavy-metal concerts hardly have beauty as an immediate or even proximate goal.

In this connection, it must be said that much harm has been done by attempts (only intermittently successful) to distill one essential Christian ideal for art — most notably in the insistence on the criterion of simplicity, coupled with restraint. Traditionally, many theological and liturgical shapers of Christian music over the centuries have sought to curtail musical excitement and ecstasy, not only because of what has been alleged to be bodily indulgence and emotional excess but also because of the perceived danger that any excessive beauty of the artistry would call attention to itself rather than serve the liturgy and God. No artistic guideline has been more common than "beautiful simplicity" in the sphere of religious aesthetics, whether Occidental or Oriental. While the rationale is plain, it clearly ignores other valid artistic possibilities. This is evident from the fact that the principle of restraint is transgressed in practice by much of the most resonant religious art and music — Monteverdi's *Vespers of the Blessed Virgin,* Mahler's *Resur-*

25. See, for example, *The Grotesque in Art and Literature,* ed. James Luther Adams and Wilson Yates (Grand Rapids: William B. Eerdmans, 1997).

rection Symphony, Mexican Baroque churches, and the shining gilded domes seen on many Russian and Eastern churches.

Musically, religious calls for artistic restraint have often translated into wanting to make sure that the textures and structures of the music do not render the words unintelligible. At the Council of Trent, for example, objections were raised to polyphony because of its tendency to obscure the sacred text with overlapping musical lines and parts. Similarly, Jewish cantors have periodically been cautioned against ostentation and a florid vocal style that might detract from sung prayer. Again, the Lutheran theologian Dietrich Bonhoeffer advocates restraint and purity in congregational singing:

> Because it is bound wholly to the Word, the singing of the congregation . . . is essentially singing in unison. . . . The purity of unison singing, unaffected by alien motives of musical techniques, the clarity, unspoiled by the attempt to give musical art an autonomy of its own apart from the words, the simplicity and frugality, the humaneness and warmth of this way of singing: [this] is the essence of all congregational singing.[26]

My point is not that such restraint can't make for good art. It is that, if applied exclusively (as is often advocated), an emphasis on artistic modesty and beautiful simplicity leaves out a vast amount of Western art and music that might otherwise be considered extremely good for religion. It also would negate the religious value of much of the best indigenous and popular religious music around the world, much of which is rhythmic, lively, effusive, or ecstatic.

There is a final point related to the widely employed criterion of simplicity. Today the emphasis on artistic modesty and simplicity has, in many churches, been changed into an emphasis on accessibility, which usually implies easy enjoyment. This has happened in "mainline" Christianity as well as in more evangelical circles. Marcus Borg, in his recent book *The Heart of Christianity: Rediscovering a Life of Faith,* describes the arts used in worship as providing a sacred context,

26. Dietrich Bonhoeffer, *Life Together* (London: SCM Press, 1954), p. 50.

a so-called thin place in the positive sense, in which the boundary between oneself, God, and the world momentarily disappears.[27] Worship, he says, allows the sacred to become present to us; it provides a
means or occasion of grace. When Borg describes the congregational
songs that are best for worship, however, all he can say is that they
combine two features: words that move us and music that can be easily sung.[28] What he fails to consider is that music that is easily sung can
sound trivial, and that one might want to cultivate a congregation's
ability to be moved by (or at least to be receptive to) more complex
musical gifts. Borg would not think of insisting, after all, that the only
Scripture ever worth pondering together in church would be something easily grasped. That would certainly exclude many of the parables of Jesus, which Borg studies intently as a New Testament scholar.
In short, some truths are difficult, and some religious states are not
easily entered. An art that erases all difficulty in the name of providing
accessibility can transgress profound religious norms and falsify what
religion needs to reveal in its perplexity and complexity.

The contemporary religious reluctance to embrace more challenging forms of good art returns us to our central question: Can especially
good art ever be especially good for Christian worship, and in part because of its goodness as art? And the answer I have been proposing is
clearly "Yes," but with qualifications. Not all good art (whether "high
art" or popular) is good in the same way or for the same communities.
Not all good art intends to be beautiful or to be appreciated for its
own sake. And not all good art that is spiritually or religiously edifying
is good in the context of worship. Yet we can say that the wide range
of art that is rightly regarded as good does offer remarkable gifts liturgically and spiritually — gifts that inferior arts cannot offer in the
same degree, and may at times even subvert. Among those good gifts
of art (listed abstractly and very selectively) are these: beautiful and

27. Marcus Borg, *The Heart of Christianity: Rediscovering a Life of Faith* (San Francisco: HarperSanFrancisco, 2004), p. 157. As in Warren's case, I situate this discussion of
Borg in the context of a theology of worship music in Chapter 6 in this volume, "Religious Music and Secular Music: A Calvinist Perspective, Re-formed."

28. Borg, *The Heart of Christianity*, pp. 156, 157.

vivid form (possibly illuming life and glorifying God), imaginative depth, expressive vitality (perhaps conveying ineffable joy in life before God), a transformative sense of sublimity and mystery, provocative questioning and exploration (of sin and suffering), evocative surprise (hidden in the everyday), meditative stillness — and ever-new ways of relating religious stories that are life-renewing. Beyond that is the fundamental role of aesthetic imagination in opening oneself to other beings, in all their particularity, and to the numinous quality of God's glory — the holy that cannot be contained or encompassed by ordinary modes of thought. Artistry and aesthetic imagination can thus become means by which we are addressed and engaged fully, as spiritually embodied creatures.

To think in this vein about the potential assets of artistry at its best may bring some sadness to go along with a large measure of gratitude. For it gives us some cause to lament the fact that artistry within religious communities in the West over the past couple of hundred years or more has, in many respects, been in decline. That widespread phenomenon is well attested, and has been discouraging to many people aesthetically attuned to religion and to spirituality as mediated artistically. Robert Wuthnow's first study of artistry and religion, *Creative Spirituality: The Way of the Artist,* while generally no less positive in tone than his more recent *All in Sync,* documents frequent perceptions of disjunction between the church and the creative arts in our own time.[29] For those who perceive themselves as called to worship in a way that is significantly artistic and aesthetic, the church's frequent disregard for disciplined and elevated arts — and a corresponding disregard for the church on the part of many artists — is a loss. That it has often been accompanied by an equal loss of probing and nuanced theological reflection has not helped matters.

Gregory the Great commented many centuries ago that the Scriptures provide water in which lambs may walk and elephants may

29. Wuthnow, *Creative Spirituality*. See, for example, his discussion of the views of Richard Rodriguez and Tony Kushner regarding art, spirituality, and the church, pp. 139-200.

swim. In recent decades Christianity seems to have been doing a lot for the lambs by providing popular and accessible arts. When it comes to artistic depth within Christian worship, perhaps it is also time to do something more for the elephants.

Christian Music:
More than Just the Words

Everyone who cares about such things has noticed that Christian music these days is continually pushing up to, and across, the boundaries of what various churches and denominations formerly regarded as acceptable. The introduction (or rejection) of new styles of music in worship — often styles associated with secular popular culture — has become both a symbol and a manifestation of the extent and character of a given church's cultural relevance and "outreach." For that very reason, however, I have been suggesting in this book that it has become increasingly important, with regard to music (and other arts), for churches to become not only more inclusive and diverse but also more discerning and discriminating (in a positive sense).

That is none too easy, as it turns out. Seldom do those two desiderata — acceptance of greater diversity and cultivation of greater discernment — move in a precisely synchronized fashion. The church goes through periods of indulgence and experimentation in its music; it also goes through what can seem like eons of reaction and restriction, of tighter and tighter regulation of music and musicians. Not infrequently, as in eighteenth-century England and in North America today, the majority of the musical diversifiers and popularizers belong to different churches, or worship at different times, from the people who see themselves as especially concerned about musical appropriateness and quality. The proponents of diversity may win converts by placing a premium on music that is immediately accessible and easily remembered (and relatively unvaried, after all). The proponents of discernment may win support by defending the status quo, which in actuality may have little to do with either aesthetic or theological perspicacity. Questions can be raised on both sides — the side that advocates baptizing every form of music that seems likeable, and the side that, in opposition, insists on excluding from worship every kind of music that doesn't present impeccable credentials from the start.

In any case, it appears that Christians need to find a more harmonious and less volatile relationship between action and reflection, musically speaking. For that to happen, we probably need to have a better understanding of worship and of what liturgical scholars such as John Witvliet and Don Saliers have termed "liturgical aesthetics." But we also need to have a better understanding of music. Because so much Christian music employs words, it is fitting that song texts receive the attention they do, even if more attention could well be paid to literary qualities. As we will see, however, discernment in Christian music means going beyond just the words, important as those may be, and giving due consideration to music's own ways of being religious.

A Case of the Psalms

Sometimes it helps to take an extreme case. In seminary classes and church workshops over a number of years, I have been asking groups to reflect on one particular example of ostensibly religious music with a supposedly sacred text — an example seemingly so askew, so obviously off the mark, that it might seem to defy even the most inclusive liturgical embrace. Composed in 1990, this is my own metrical psalm, a paraphrase of Psalm 23 to be sung to the tune of "Rudolph the Red-Nosed Reindeer."

I Know the Lord's My Shepherd
(Lyrics: Frank Burch Brown, © 1990)

(Tune: Rudolph the Red-Nosed Reindeer)

I know the Lord's my shepherd;
I won't ever need a thing.
He gives me grass that's greenest;
Takes me to the coolest spring.

When I am sad he cheers me;
When I'm bad he makes me good.
Wherever he will lead me,
I will follow as I should.

> Though I walk through valleys
> Dark as death and sin,
> Nothing there can frighten me;
> With your staff you're my true friend.

People can see I'm fed well;
I could hardly ask for more.
I'm going to stay forever
With the one who's really Lord!

In sharing this psalm with various church groups and seminary classes — and sometimes with Jewish students — I have found that the discussion typically concentrates first on the words, and on what, if anything, is the matter with them. Words, after all, usually occupy the focal awareness of worshipers engaged in singing. One thing that people familiar with hymnody note immediately about the text is that, being a metrical psalm, it conforms at one level to a long tradition. As is well known, the Reformed churches, and the Church of England until the nineteenth century, traditionally prescribed the singing of psalms instead of hymns of merely "human composure." Because psalms straight from the Bible are unrhymed and irregular in meter, vast numbers of metered and rhymed psalms were produced in order to facilitate singing. One can compare the present version with other, more venerable metrical paraphrases of the same psalm, such as "My Shepherd Will Supply My Need" (Isaac Watts) and "The King of Love My Shepherd Is" (Henry Williams Baker).

Although discussants have no trouble spotting things about the new text that are worrisome, they often, and before long, devise ways to find the words somehow fitting. Gestalt psychologists confirmed some time ago the human propensity to make sense of patterns that might at first seem incongruous or nonsensical — such as the array of ink blots used in Rorschach tests. It is perhaps to be expected, therefore, that even people who might otherwise feel critical can soon find themselves imagining ways in which this text can be "saved." They may observe that the text does, after all, capture most of the plain sense of the original psalm; that it is singable and easily memorized; that it might be a good way to introduce children to the psalm; and so forth.

When the discussion shifts to the music, people freely admit to a sense of amusement. But they quickly find nice things to say about the tune as well. For one thing, virtually everyone agrees that my metrical paraphrase and the newly recruited psalm tune "Rudolph" are in some sense a good match. Certainly, the music matches the bright, cheerful, and singsongy qualities of my verse.

But therein lies the problem, of course. As some people are sure to point out sooner or later, the music can be heard as reinforcing the trivializing tendencies already in evidence in the verses of "I Know the Lord's My Shepherd." This is prancing and dancing music, with scarcely a cloud in its melodic and harmonic sky. Just as my verbal rendition of the psalm extinguishes any sobering thoughts that might arise when walking through valleys dark as death, the music at that very point has us imagine a pleasant valley detour that is little more than a lark.

A Puzzling Acceptance

And so it has come as a surprise to me, and frankly something of a shock, to find that, with every passing year, a larger and larger proportion of good Christian folk end up wanting to embrace both the words and the music of "I Know the Lord's My Shepherd." How to account for this phenomenon? Answering that question entails some consideration of changes in ideals for worship; but it also entails acknowledgment of possible changes in ideals and ideas of music itself.

The increasing eagerness to welcome such verbal levity and musical lightness as I've arranged in my test case appears to be accompanied by an ever-greater willingness to be playful and, indeed, entertaining with worship in general. It is characteristic of the trend that, as I recently observed in person, one can now witness an adult baptism in which the pastor, while standing in the baptistery prior to immersing a well-tanned man (and later the man's wife and children), freely jokes that he wishes he could baptize the man's golf clubs as well. This move toward casual levity is supported by an increasingly emphatic insistence throughout much of Christian culture on what might be called irrepressible optimism — the sense that to acknowledge the deep darkness of the shadows or the possible starkness of death itself is to be fundamentally unfaithful; the sense that praise is the alpha and omega of worship, and that the only proper praise is happy praise.

Perhaps that happy optimism — a far cry from the Calvinism of an earlier era — is one reason why many Christians of various stripes are so ready to come to the defense of the music of "Rudolph" as in some way fitting for Christian worship, considered in a certain light. Some point out how the story of Rudolph the reindeer with his glowing red nose is itself a miniature tale of rejection and exaltation. Others even read the Rudolph story Christologically — the despised and rejected reindeer who becomes redeemer and spiritual leader in the end, his light guiding his followers to heights of blessing. Whether any of that sense of the story gets into the music itself is doubtful, but it's not a question that troubles these particular interlocutors.

While theologians may well worry about a Christian optimism that goes so far as to make light of all trials and tribulations, we should notice that there are nevertheless some reasons, better reasons, for not wanting instantly to rule out using "I Know the Lord's My Shepherd" in Christian worship — even if, in the end, we need to be able to discern how that allegiance is likewise quite questionable in some respects (as I shall soon argue).

First, sociologically speaking, music increasingly has a kind of social identification. And "Rudolph" in any case is identified strongly with children, a group that has frequently been excluded from full participation in worship (whatever the reasons for that may be). Consequently, some people involved in Christian education have a special motivation for accepting and promoting the religious value of this music as a psalm tune, even though it might otherwise never occur to them to do so. (Some others equally committed to education may find the music all the more unacceptable in church, fearing that it sells children short.)

Speaking more generally, we can say that church leaders have acknowledged more and more that there are legitimate reasons for every major group to have its preferred forms of music represented in worship. This musical representation of a wide range of social identities encourages what post–Vatican II Catholics in particular call "full, conscious, and active participation." The social identification of musical styles is thus becoming a virtually unavoidable factor in determining what is indeed appropriate in a given musical and liturgical context. Even the question of musical quality (of "good music" as distinct from music "good for worship") evidently cannot be divorced entirely from consideration of whose music it is to begin with, and who knows most about its possible value.

But how could music that seems trivial and lightly entertaining ever seem good for worship, whatever the music's social affinities? Well, in this case, the music could seem significant precisely *because* of its lightness — when heard in a certain way and with certain groups in mind. Music is not only the sounds our ears hear; it is also what we hear *in* those sounds: what our minds make of the sounds. What we hear in music — what the music seems to express, its mood, its qualities or beauty — is (like so much else) partly socially constructed. Children and their advocates may be inclined to hear *in* this music something that others might tune out or ignore — perhaps an overtone of hopeful childhood experience that still needs protection from shadows and that is happy to be included in worship.

The implications of such issues go well beyond whether it is ever acceptable to use a relatively playful or silly metrical psalm in worship. They have to do with how music is heard and received more broadly. Many British folk tunes, such as "Forest Green," along with ancient and venerable hymns of the church, such as "Old One Hundredth," sounded inspiring and even exemplary to Ralph Vaughan Williams in his job as music editor of the *English Hymnal* in the early years of the twentieth century. Many of us would say he was right in what he approved for inclusion. But in retrospect one might argue that he was unduly inattentive to the worship potential of certain other kinds of music. One thinks of music from the former British colonies in particular — North American, Caribbean, African, Indian — some of which sounds, to be sure, more exuberant and rhythmic than might at first have seemed proper for worship when judged by the standards then associated with the Church of England.

All the factors we have been reviewing serve to remind us that context is important to the meaning and function of many — perhaps most — kinds of music. Although music — at least some kinds of music — can communicate marvelously across cultures, its inner character is often revealed fully only through familiarity and adept interpretation; music is by no means a universal language in the sense often assumed.

In the end, however, Christian practical theologians, musicians, and worship leaders need to be able to question certain musical values as they emerge within local contexts and the church at large. If our goal is to become at once more inclusive and more discerning, we must learn to test the spirit at work in music itself. One can accept almost any musical offering under special circumstances, but that only gets one so far. It is very different from establishing expectations and criteria that one hopes can become audible to most relatively astute listeners in the process of comparative listening, even if rarely specifiable in words alone.

Renewed Discernment

Accordingly, while acknowledging why one might conceivably welcome "I Know the Lord's My Shepherd" into worship in a limited way, we need to return now to the earlier, initial impression that the music itself somehow goes against the grain of the psalm it purports to render anew. That impression, while qualified by the contrary testimony we have considered, takes on new life when one tries to imagine "Rudolph" as a setting not of my own metrical paraphrase but of the King James Version of the Twenty-third Psalm. Because that classic translation is not metrical, and therefore not susceptible to being sung to regularly metered music such as "Rudolph," one possible procedure is to read the King James text as a "voice-over," with a small group humming the tune of "Rudolph" in the background.

When that is done, the singers who are humming the tune underneath the reading of the psalm inevitably slow down the tempo and try to make the music more legato. Yet it is virtually impossible to perceive even a softer, slower, smoother rendition of "Rudolph" as either reverent or uplifting, or as consistent in any other way with the tenor or core concerns of the Twenty-third Psalm. After all, this psalm, even if it makes no explicit reference to death (if one follows some alternative translations), does contemplate walking by God's help through the deepest of shadows, and thus rightly figures in many a funeral service.

Such an attempt to accompany the veritably classic version of the Twenty-third Psalm with the music of "Rudolph" will leave little doubt that the reindeer music — the music itself — stays in a much lower orbit than the poetry of Psalm 23. In fact, if one free-associates with the music as it is hummed, one readily discerns that the music expresses a register of feeling that goes much better with holiday escapades and shopping sprees than with private devotion or public prayer. Even after one gives all due credit to the social construction of musical meaning, it must be said that this music is not, after all, infinitely malleable or suited to all purposes.

That comes as no great surprise, to be sure. But if it is true, it gives us reason to question the premises of those whose promotion of new church music requires just two things: (1) that the music have scriptural or Christian words; and (2) that the music be immediately appealing. We can now see clearly that both criteria are inadequate, in different ways. Each fails to take into account how the artistic medium shapes the message, and thus both ignore a cardinal principle of aesthetics: In art the *message* can never be separated entirely from the *medium* conveying and shaping it. Thus, in the case of my "Rudolph" version of Psalm 23, the first criterion is inadequate for selecting good worship music because, even though the plain sense of my metrical psalm is in some way scriptural, the verse is such doggerel that it sinks far below the aesthetic beauty of the Twenty-third Psalm itself — an aesthetic defect that is also a religious flaw, both theological and liturgical. The second criterion is likewise inadequate because, even if "Rudolph" has its musical appeal, the tone and character of the music sound relatively frivolous to most listeners and, in any case, are incongruous with the tone and character of the scriptural words the tune accompanies and should complement. Even if we concede that religion can have its moments of legitimate frivolity, the Twenty-third Psalm invites nothing of the sort. The music thus fails the poetry and purpose of the Scripture, and in that way fails in a potentially sacred calling. Any religion that cannot survive such artistic failures will not, of course, survive for long, particularly since no form of expression is perfectly adequate to the highest religious realities. By the same token, however, any kind of religion that consistently fails to find a fitting voice (artistic and otherwise) for the sort of transformative faith expressed in the Twenty-third Psalm is itself in danger of failing in its own highest calling.

What does all this mean for our search for spiritual and aesthetic discernment to go along with musical acceptance and diversification? None of what has been observed here is meant to deny that some music is relatively adaptable and that the line between sacred and secular style is constantly and rightly being crossed or redrawn. Few music theorists or practitioners of liturgical music would say, for example, what the Catholic Church frequently taught in the past: that the piano is an inherently secular instrument that has no place in worship.

Equally few would insist, along with John Calvin (following Plato), that certain kinds of music are invariably worshipful or spiritually healthy, while other kinds are invariably degrading or unhealthy, with each kind of music definitely affecting soul and body for good or ill.

At the same time, there is no reason to deny, in the end, that different kinds of music do have different powers and effects and that certain musical gestures, and indeed whole compositions, are more fitting to a given religious purpose than others are. Moreover, it is now more necessary than ever to affirm something that the church has seldom clearly recognized: Music itself — and not least in the context of worship — has its own ways of interpreting the very meaning of faith, prayer, and praise. The better forms of music go some places where words alone cannot. Even those whose ears are untrained can nonetheless learn to hear what the Spirit is saying musically as well as verbally.

As for those who would like musically suitable psalms for children, the better answer is surely not to turn to "I Know the Lord's My Shepherd," but to seek out something more creative and vital, perhaps something newly composed. Maybe it will be music from a composer good at making old traditions sound new, just as a familiar psalm can become new again in the very act of singing it, all the days of our lives.

CHAPTER 6

Religious Music and Secular Music: A Calvinist Perspective, Re-formed

Why Calvin?

In our time, many Christians have encountered more kinds of music in church than previous generations would normally have encountered in all the spheres of life combined — secular as well as sacred. The contrast with Calvin's expectations could not be greater. For Calvin rejected virtually every kind of church music other than unison, vernacular, unaccompanied psalm-singing by the congregation. Calvin's practical theology of music is thus likely to appear profoundly unfashionable. But despite that fact, or perhaps precisely because of it, it may be that we can begin to see his position from a new perspective, along with some of its liturgical and cultural implications that might be especially pertinent to any attempt today to be not only inclusive but also discerning with respect to music and the church.

The effort to restore an awareness of Calvin's theology of music is not new, of course. In 1951, Charles Garside began an article on Calvin and music with a complaint that, despite a recent renascence of Calvin studies, Calvin's views on art and music were still either neglected or else misunderstood and unfairly maligned. Garside in his brief article offered a balanced picture, at least with respect to Calvin's appraisal of music in his Preface to the Genevan Psalter, as pub-

99

lished in 1542 and 1543. Garside followed up with a longer, though still succinct, monograph on Calvin's theology of music,[1] in which he took more account of earlier scholarship.[2] Thanks to the research of Garside and others — including, most recently, scholars such as John Witvliet and Jeffrey VanderWilt[3] — one cannot fairly complain that Calvin's judgments regarding music have never received scholarly attention.

Yet one would never guess, from most other discussions of Calvin and his influence, that Calvin had a distinctive theological approach to music, or that, in the words of the music historian Paul Henry Lang, "The Huguenot [Genevan] Psalter became, in both its textual and its musical forms, an inalienable part of Protestant music and exerted a tremendous influence on all of Protestant Europe and the American colonies."[4]

To be sure, Calvin's musical legacy was ambiguous. Few Presbyterians today would have any interest in reviving worship and music in a rigorously Genevan mode. And there is some truth to Lang's observation that "the countries which accepted the doctrines of Calvinism — Scotland, where John Knox implanted them, some parts of Holland and Switzerland, and the New England states — did not excel in [art music] once these doctrines became an essential factor in their life."

1. Charles Garside, *The Origins of Calvin's Theology of Music: 1536-1543*, Transactions of the American Philosophical Society, vol. 69, pt. 4 (Philadelphia: American Philosophical Society, 1979).

2. Garside's fuller discussion takes into consideration Émile Doumergue, *L'art et le sentiment dans l'oeuvre de Calvin* (Geneva: Slatkine Reprints, 1970) — three lectures, the first of which is translated as "Music in the Work of Calvin," *Princeton Theological Review* 7 (Oct. 1909): 329-52; also Léon Wencelius, *L'esthétique de Calvin* (Paris: Belles Lettres, 1938); and Walter Blankenburg, "Calvin," in the encyclopedic *Die Musik in Geschichte und Gegenwart* (Kassel and Basel: Barenreiter, 1952).

3. See John D. Witvliet, "The Spirituality of the Psalter in Calvin's Geneva," in his book *Worship Seeking Understanding: Windows into Christian Practice* (Grand Rapids: Baker Academic, 2003), pp. 203-29; and Jeffrey T. VanderWilt, "John Calvin's Theology of Liturgical Song," *Christian Scholar's Review* 25 (1995): 63-82.

4. Paul Henry Lang, *Music in Western Civilization* (New York: W. W. Norton, 1941), p. 259.

Lang observes that this contrasted sharply with the "great musical culture of the followers of Luther."[5]

This chapter, accordingly, is Calvinist in spirit, but only partly so. In an endeavor to revisit Calvin in such a way as to contribute to the theology of music today, it is also re-forming in character, and ecumenical. After offering an interpretation of the practical theology of music found in Calvin, I re-examine limitations and implications of the familiar but often misconceived distinction between sacred and secular in the realm of music.

Calvin on the Use and Abuse of Music

In view of Luther's wholehearted embrace of music, most Protestant discussions of how best to cultivate the music of the church invoke Luther instead of Calvin — invariably with a reminder that Luther happily raided and adapted secular musical sources and defended the practice with the statement that he didn't want the devil to have all the good tunes. But while Luther may never have said exactly that (we don't know for sure), and while Luther had more substantial things to say theologically about music, we will see that, in relation to our central question regarding sacred and secular music, John Calvin's observations are particularly worth attending to.

In his Preface to the Psalter, written in 1542 and expanded in 1543 into what would remain his most developed statement on music, Calvin explains that public prayer is of two kinds: with words alone and with song. Of sung prayer — essentially the singing of psalms — Calvin says that in truth "we know from experience that song has great force and vigor to arouse and inflame people's hearts to invoke and praise God with a more vehement and ardent zeal."[6] After praising music in this way, however, Calvin immediately and characteristically

5. Lang, *Music in Western Civilization*, p. 257.
6. John Calvin's "Foreword [or Preface] to the Psalter," translated by Charles Garside, in *John Calvin: Writings on Pastoral Piety*, ed. Elsie Anne McKee, Classics of Western Spirituality (New York: Paulist Press, 2001), pp. 91-97; quotation on p. 94.

provides a word of caution: "There must always be concern that the song be neither light nor frivolous, but have gravity and majesty, as Saint Augustine says. And thus there is a great difference between the music which one makes to entertain people at table and in their homes, and the psalms which are sung in the church in the presence of God and His angels."[7]

One often hears it said that for Calvin, and for the Reformed tradition more generally, the distinction between sacred and secular is constantly blurred and at times erased, because God's claims are said to extend to every corner of life.[8] But when it comes to music deemed fit for worship as compared with music deemed unfit and worldly, Calvin's distinction here is sharp. Music for public worship is to have gravity and majesty, untouched by frivolity. It is music that is especially appropriate to being sung "in the presence of God and His angels."

Even so, it is not as though Calvin thinks that only church music can honor God or serve a religious function. In a lengthy passage he added in the 1543 edition of the Psalter, Calvin goes on to observe, in fact, that even singing in homes and in the fields can be done in such a way as to praise God and "rejoice in God," lifting up our hearts to God even as we are consoled by meditating on God's virtue, goodness, wisdom, and justice. While Calvin continues to distinguish between church music and music that honors God outside the church, he makes an even sharper distinction between, on the one hand, music that honors God and enhances life — whether in church or outside — and, on the other hand, music that is indulgent and vain. Specifically, Calvin goes on to distinguish between the act of rejoicing in God and the act of rejoicing in "vanity." Music can do either of those things, he suggests. And given our human nature since the Fall, Calvin says, human beings are all too ready "to look for all manner of demented and vicious rejoicing" associated with the temptations of the flesh and the

---

7. Calvin, "Foreword [or Preface] to the Psalter," p. 94.

8. See, for instance, T. Hartley Hall IV, "The Shape of Reformed Piety," in *Spiritual Traditions for the Contemporary Church,* ed. Robin Maas and Gabriel O'Donnell (Nashville: Abingdon Press, 1990), p. 209.

world — all of which contrasts with spiritual joy that God provides to distract us from those very temptations.[9]

Music, Calvin declares, is a gift of God. It is one of the main ways — perhaps the principal way — in which people find pleasure and recreation. But for that very reason, Calvin asserts, we must be careful not to abuse the gift of music. We need to be musically moderate and avoid licentiousness. We must not allow our use of music to make us (as he says, in provocatively gendered language) "effeminate in disordered delights."[10] For, as Plato observed long ago, there is "scarcely anything in the world which is more capable of turning or moving morals this way and that." In fact, Calvin argues, our experience tells us that music "has a secret and almost incredible power to arouse hearts in one way or another." We must not employ music thoughtlessly, therefore. As the "ancient doctors of the church" warned repeatedly, people can easily become addicted to "unseemly and obscene songs."[11]

Calvin makes a point of saying not only that we should avoid sinful and obscene *words* in the songs we sing but also that we should sing good, holy, and moderate *melodies*. They should be "moderated in the manner which we have adopted, to carry gravity and majesty appropriate to the subject," and even in daily life should be in some sense "suitable for singing in the church."[12] Calvin argues that we should not put melodies of any sort to bad use. For when a melody is combined with evil words, Calvin observes, it "pierces the heart that much more strongly and enters into it; just as through a funnel wine is poured into a container, so also venom and corruption are distilled to the depth of the heart by the melody."[13] Here Calvin seemingly has in the back of his mind Book Three of Plato's *Republic*, where Plato has Socrates warn against allowing sweet, soft, and melancholy music to

9. Calvin, "Foreword [or Preface] to the Psalter," p. 95.
10. Calvin, "Foreword [or Preface] to the Psalter," p. 95.
11. Calvin, "Foreword [or Preface] to the Psalter," p. 95.
12. Calvin, "Foreword [or Preface] to the Psalter," p. 97.
13. Calvin, "Foreword [or Preface] to the Psalter," p. 96.

pour into a man's soul through the funnel of his ears, since that can lead to dissipation and the enfeeblement of a potential warrior.

In making such comments, Calvin is evidently talking about music-making in general. But by now he has made church-singing almost paradigmatic for all good singing. To be sure, music in the world — at home and in the fields — can have a little more latitude in its style; we know, for example, that Calvin and his close associates permitted or encouraged religious music outside the church to be accompanied by instruments and to be harmonized, or provided with multi-voiced, polyphonic arrangements.[14] (That is evident from the various ways in which the music of the Genevan Psalter was almost immediately arranged for home use.) Calvin insists that such music outside the church has religious value, allowing us to rejoice in God. Truly worldly music is another matter, however. Worldly songs, Calvin states, are "in part empty and frivolous, in part stupid and dull, in part obscene and vile, and in consequence evil and harmful."[15]

Since Calvin goes to the trouble of distinguishing between the words of a song and its melody, we might ask whether he thinks that music alone (the melody without words) could ever be harmful. If the answer is not entirely clear, it is perhaps because Calvin, like the ancient Greeks and Romans, typically thought of music as combined with words. Even so, like Plato, he does appear to believe that music by itself can sound immoderate, disordered, dull, or frivolous. As we have seen, however, Calvin also seems to suggest that even a beautiful melody can be harmful when its words are unedifying. In that case the melody can intensify the evil effect of the words and make the text more seductive or debilitating, as though acting like a funnel for wine.

While Calvin worries about the effect of combining attractive music with dubious words, he does not discuss explicitly the effect of combining good or devout words with immoderate or trivial music. In the previous chapter, I discussed the mixed effects of a metrical psalm that I

14. See Walter Blankenburg, "Church Music in Reformed Europe," in Friedrich Blume et al., *Protestant Church Music* (London: Victor Gollancz, 1975), pp. 532-36.

15. Calvin, "Foreword [or Preface] to the Psalter," p. 97.

once composed as an experiment — a versification of Psalm 23 — to be sung to the tune of "Rudolph the Red-Nosed Reindeer." Calvin did not address that kind of thing. But it is not hard to guess what he would say, if asked. He would surely say that setting the Twenty-third Psalm to such a light and amusing tune would be indecent and unfitting, and a desecration of the sacred words. That judgment is implicit in Calvin's cautioning against using music of a frivolous sort in church.

We can see now that Calvin offers reflections on what turn out be four kinds of music: (1) music intended for church; (2) explicitly religious music outside the church; (3) secular music that, while meant for entertainment, can still be enjoyed "in God"; and, lastly, (4) thoroughly worldly music that potentially "perverts good morals," as he says, and that leads away from God. In the process, Calvin states or implies several criteria for what would be good music from a Christian point of view — good for church and good for use in the wider world.

Secular Music as an Endangered Species

Before we try to flesh out Calvin's theological criteria and their musical implications, we need to ponder the possibility that, according to Calvin at his most "advanced," there is really no room in Christian life and culture, after all, for secular music, or at least for secular song. Charles Garside, who underscores this conclusion, was perhaps the first scholar to notice a pronounced shift in emphasis between the 1542 text of the Preface to the Psalter, with its primary concern for church music as such, and the 1543 text, which adds material that is concerned more with music outside the church. Garside spells out his interpretation of what this shift means in his brief monograph titled *The Origins of Calvin's Theology of Music,* where he traces three stages in Calvin's thinking about music between 1536 and 1543. Garside takes into account several successive editions of the *Institutes of the Christian Religion* as well as signal documents such as Calvin's "Articles concerning the Organization of the Church and of Worship at Geneva" (1937) and, most decisively, both the original and the expanded versions of Calvin's Preface to the Psalter. What is most relevant to our purpose is a trajectory summed up succinctly by Garside himself: "Hesitant at first to admit music to worship, later granting to psalmody an indispensable place in the liturgy, Calvin proposes [in the final version of the Preface] that even outside the liturgy only the psalms be sung."[16] Whether Calvin also wants to jettison purely instrumental music from secular life is unknown, Garside observes. Calvin never discusses purely instrumental music.

If Garside is right about this shift in Calvin's thought, and it seems he is, one important result is this:

> The distinction between the secular and the sacred which Calvin had been at such pains to establish in 1542 is to be obliterated, for he looks now to the eventual elimination of all secular vocal music. In the ideal future, when men and women sang, not only at public worship, but in their private prayers and everywhere else, even in their entertainment "at table and in their homes," they would sing only the "divine and celestial hymns" of David.[17]

How literally are we to take Calvin here? How far, and how fast, did he really want to go in promoting a life and musical culture devoted entirely to the psalms? There is ample evidence that, in his day and later, Calvinist musicians and poets poured enormous energy and a certain amount of creativity into all sorts of psalm settings for use in the world at large, and not only in church.[18] But one is tempted to conclude that Calvin, in promoting his new Psalter, did not think through all the possible consequences or details. Envisioning how edifying his psalter could be in everyday life — and disgusted by what he referred to as the "lascivious and obscene ditties" associated with dance and the like[19] — he could only picture its well-nigh ubiquitous value.

16. Garside, *The Origins of Calvin's Theology of Music*, p. 24.

17. Garside, *The Origins of Calvin's Theology of Music*, p. 25.

18. Blankenburg, "Church Music in Reformed Europe," in Blume et al., *Protestant Church Music*, p. 544.

19. John Calvin, Memorandum to the Synod of Zürich (May 1538), quoted in Garside, *The Origins of Calvin's Theology of Music*, p. 24.

Garside thinks that this fixation on the psalms in all of life is a consistent, if extreme, outgrowth of the Protestant principle of *sola scriptura*.[20] But whether Calvin actually felt sure that the New Testament Christians sang nothing but psalms when making music at home or at weddings or in harvesting crops, it is impossible to know. In any case, Garside traces Calvin's change of mind and heart to the Lutheran Martin Bucer and to Augustine, whose *Confessions* Calvin had been reading. Partly under Bucer's influence in Strasburg, Calvin had already experienced, and been impressed by, congregational song — particularly the singing of psalms and biblical canticles (which Calvin was likewise to approve as essentially psalm-like). Bucer, like Calvin after him, had advocated using only Scripture-based songs and prayers, translated into the vernacular. Bucer had also set a precedent for Calvin in emphasizing the importance of understanding the words of what is sung, and in all this believed that one would only be following the example of the "ancient holy fathers" of the church.[21] It is not surprising, therefore, to discover that Bucer in 1542 had already declared, ahead of Calvin, that "all singing and playing (which above all things are capable of moving our spirits powerfully and ardently) should be used in no other way except for sacred praise, prayer, teaching, and admonition. . . . Absolutely no song and no instrumentalizing may be sung and used except by and for Christian spiritual activities."[22]

Yet in the end Calvin sounds, if anything, even more austere than Bucer in the regulation of music. One major difference is that Lutherans like Bucer saw different genres implied in the three terms "Psalms," "hymns," and "spiritual songs" found in Ephesians 5:19, and accordingly embraced hymns and religious songs composed by postbiblical poets.

As Garside points out, Calvin's austerity also derived from his recent reading of Book Ten of Augustine's *Confessions*. There Augustine worried about the emotional impact of the songs he had sung in

20. Garside, *The Origins of Calvin's Theology of Music*, p. 29.

21. Garside, *The Origins of Calvin's Theology of Music*, pp. 11-12.

22. Quoted and translated by Garside, *The Origins of Calvin's Theology of Music*, p. 30.

church, and expressed his determination to avoid the temptation to dwell on the beauty of the music rather than on the truth of the sacred words themselves. Indeed, Augustine, for all his love of music, could barely bring himself to approve of singing in church. That distrust of the seductive power of music as such, along with the absolute priority that Augustine placed on the sacred text, only reinforced the new, humanistic tendency within Calvin and others of his time to insist that music serve the words, rather than the other way around. And in Calvin's view the best words, religiously, would surely be biblical. When we sing the words of the psalms, Calvin argues in his Preface to the Psalter, "we are certain that God puts the words in our mouths, as if He Himself were singing in us to exalt His glory. Wherefore Chrysostom exhorts men as well as women and little children to accustom themselves to sing them, in order that this may be, as it were, a meditation for associating themselves with the company of angels."[23]

In view of all this, lovers of music, both religious and secular, may feel by now that I have done Calvin no favors by revisiting his views. Even Bucer, it may seem, comes off better — not to mention Luther, whose musical legacy would eventually include J. S. Bach, among many others. While sympathetic to that claim, I want to show that Calvin's distinctive emphasis, however off-putting to lovers of music, does call attention to significant assets and dangers of music that one might easily miss in Luther's more sweeping embrace of musical culture. It is to these features that we now turn, before concluding with a more general appraisal.

Reclaiming and Reforming Calvin's Theology of Music

Even more than Bucer, and far more than Luther, Calvin insisted on the importance of developing a style of music that was distinctly sacred. And in this he seems to have succeeded. According to Walter Blankenburg, Calvin through his psalter (which became enormously

23. Calvin, "Foreword [or Preface] to the Psalter," p. 96.

popular) was responsible for developing a Protestant musical *stilus ecclesiasticus,* much as Palestrina might be said to have developed a correspondingly Catholic one.[24] Much research has gone into tracking down sources of, and influences on, the tunes of the psalms as found in the Genevan Psalter. While the results are somewhat inconclusive, many of the composers and arrangers of the tunes are known (the most famous being Louis or Loys Bourgeois). And there seems to be widespread agreement that each tune was reworked specifically for the Psalter. Some of the tunes are modeled on Gregorian chant, or at least use church modes, whereas a relatively small number have secular models.[25] Moreover, when arranged polyphonically by composers such as Claude Goudimel and Louis Bourgeois, the psalm motets based on the Genevan Psalter became, in Blankenburg's phrase, "among the most important creations of Protestant church music."[26]

All in all, therefore, the Genevan Psalter in its different uses and arrangements provided different ways of ushering the heart and soul into one state or another before God. When arranged for use in the world, the sung Psalter would allow the Calvinist to pray without ceasing — through memorized song that would pervade life in home and field.[27] When further purified and sanctified through special unison, unaccompanied singing in church, the Psalms would more fully and directly lift up the heart to God, a phrase of Calvin's that surely alludes to the *Sursum corda* of communion liturgies.

What motivated Calvin's insistence on a style of church music that would be strikingly different from secular styles and noticeably different from psalm settings in the world? Jeffrey VanderWilt provides one key theological motivation when he connects Calvin's musical aesthetic with a desire to protect the majesty and sovereignty of God. "For Calvin," he writes, "one would better keep one's mouth silent and one's tongue still than to trivialize the music of the Church's worship by the singing of clever tunes. The results of such were, for him,

24. Blankenburg, "Calvin," *Die Musik in Geschichte und Gegenwart,* p. 665.
25. Blankenburg, "Church Music in Reformed Europe," pp. 522-23.
26. Blankenburg, "Church Music in Reformed Europe," p. 535.
27. Calvin, "Foreword [or Preface] to the Psalter," p. 96.

disastrous: impotent and sterile worship, the corruption of the soul, and finally, the dishonoring of God."[28]

Calvin also seems to have been convinced, however, that the texts of the psalms are capable of encompassing the full range of human feeling. In his Preface to his *Commentary on the Psalms,* Calvin speaks of the book of Psalms as an "Anatomy of All the Parts of the Soul," because there is allegedly no possible human emotion that is not mirrored there — pains, sorrows, fears, doubts, hopes, cares, anxieties.[29] It seems to follow that, for Calvin, the singing of the psalms would be a way of receiving God's accommodation to our humanity and infirmity.

But if that is the case — if God reaches out to the full range of human feeling and experience through the psalms — why not meet that outreach musically by drawing on the full range of existing styles, both secular as well as religious? Why not, in that very way, help bring our whole humanity into worship, with all our different modes of expression and diverse moods? Could it not also be part of our calling to compose and sing music that is as varied as the people and communities who lift their hearts to God in song?

My own answer to that last question would be a qualified "Yes." The evidence suggests that Calvin seriously overestimates the capacity of a narrowly limited repertoire of musical styles to express a full range of human experience, and indeed to do justice to the full capacity of worship itself. And in this regard he is overly fearful or negligent of God's gifts in secular culture. The only references to secular music in Calvin seem to be to tunes (and words) that he immediately criticizes in one way or another as "in part empty and frivolous, in part stupid and dull, in part obscene and vile, and in consequence evil and harmful."[30] That hardly does justice to the richness of secular music available in Renaissance Europe, particularly as greater and greater emphasis was placed on the capacity of music to interpret texts and to

28. VanderWilt, "John Calvin's Theology of Liturgical Song," p. 75.

29. John Calvin, Preface to the Commentary on the Psalms, in *The Piety of John Calvin,* trans. and ed. Ford Lewis Battles (Grand Rapids: Baker Book House, 1978), pp. 27-28.

30. Calvin, "Foreword [or Preface] to the Psalter," p. 97.

express the relevant emotions. Moreover, I cannot find a single passage in Calvin in which he unequivocally acknowledges (as Martin Luther and Augustine both do) the God-given value of beautiful music as such, of music as harmoniously ordered sound — whether or not accompanied by religious words.

Nevertheless, Calvin sees music as integral to a whole life that one can "enjoy in God," even in the world.[31] And he insists ardently that music is intrinsic to public worship. He will not let music be used uncritically in either case.

The implications of that last point for present-day practice are not hard to discern. Calvin would never accept the assumption that every form of music that human beings find somehow pleasurable is healthy and good, let alone good for worship, since in his view there is nothing that is untouched by sin, and no powerful medium that cannot be abused. In that respect, I believe, Calvin helps us re-introduce an important critical note in a culture that has long specialized in secular music of every sort — especially in its most commercial forms — and in which churches now find themselves eagerly absorbing and adapting virtually every style from the world outside (the reverse of what Calvin desired).

Calvin would certainly question, for example, the reasoning in the passage from Rick Warren that we examined in a previous chapter. I am again referring to the place in *The Purpose Driven Life* where Warren writes, "Worship has nothing to do with the style or volume or speed of a song. God loves all kinds of music because he invented it all — fast and slow, loud and soft, old and new. You probably don't like it all, but God does! If it is offered to God in spirit and truth, it is an act of worship."[32] Such a statement, welcoming as it is, forgets entirely that certain kinds of music may be driven — whether by nature or by culture and "social construction" — toward feelings and outlooks far

31. The idea of enjoying music or art "in God" is consistent with Calvin but is a concept I have derived, myself, from Augustine and biblical principles. See my *Good Taste, Bad Taste, and Christian Taste: Aesthetics in Religious Life* (New York: Oxford University Press, 2000), pp. 111-20.

32. Rick Warren, *The Purpose Driven Life* (Grand Rapids: Zondervan, 2002), p. 65.

removed from either Christian worship or the Christian life in general. To offer all kinds of music to God as an act of worship would be misguided, because much music, if one is listening, is evocative of something quite different — the lightest sort of entertainment, for instance, or a fervently erotic atmosphere. While our judgments need to take contexts and communities into account, and while much music is amenable to multiple sorts of uses, every kind of music tends to have a particular "tone of voice" that it is unwise to ignore.

We have also taken note of a common liberal or "mainline" counterpart to Warren's sort of evangelical yet uncritical welcoming of whatever music people happen to like. This alternative approach, exemplified by the thinking of Marcus Borg, likewise sells music short, even though it nominally expects more from music in worship — not just pleasing or even riveting sounds, but a sense of the sacred. I am returning to Borg's brief acknowledgment of music in his book *The Heart of Christianity: Rediscovering a Life of Faith:* "More Protestants report being moved by hymn singing than by any other element in the service. We sing to God, and our hearts are opened. The hymns that do this best combine two features: words that move us and music that can be easily sung."[33] Borg resembles Calvin in placing great emphasis on the words that are sung, which he identifies as something that can move us. What is missing here is Calvin's clear desire for the music itself to be fitting and uplifting, so that in the act of singing, we are brought into the "presence of God and the angels." At the same time, Calvin is plainly more aware than Borg appears to be that a song that is merely easy to sing can sometimes sound insipid, trite, or — what is worse — sacrilegious.

I return, therefore, to the Calvinist principle that, however rich the resources of secular music — and after several centuries now of intense cultivation, they have become far richer than Calvin ever imagined — the church must be attentive to values that enable at least some music to lift us worshipfully into the presence of God and the angels. To ig-

33. Marcus Borg, *The Heart of Christianity: Rediscovering a Life of Faith* (San Francisco: HarperSanFrancisco, 2004), p. 157.

nore the different powers of music in this regard is as myopic as ignoring the different uses and powers of architecture, and of language itself. Thus the church must be discerning as it searches for music that, in the larger culture, gives voice to human feelings and transformative beauty, with or without words, and in a way that can likewise be enjoyed in God, and offered up to God.

Both directly and indirectly, Calvin's approach to music can help us remember that music does not in reality divide neatly into just two kinds, religious and secular. There is church music, such as the singing of psalms. And there is music that employs religious texts and serves religious ends in the world outside the church, such as in the home or in concert. There is also music that is indirectly religious (or spiritual) in that it enhances and enriches our enjoyment of life in a manner blessed by God, but without specific religious words or goals. Such music we enjoy "in God," without addressing it to God. Although Calvin himself never talked explicitly about such music, its existence receives vivid attestation in the Calvinist Karl Barth's whimsical but also serious speculation that, in heaven, the angels in praising God play Bach (wonderful and mostly "religious" music) but that, when playing for their own enjoyment, they play Mozart (wonderful and mostly "secular" music) — whereupon God likewise listens in with pleasure.[34] Finally, there is music that has little or no connection with the religious ends of life and that in some circumstances can indulge emotions and inculcate attitudes in conflict with the life to which God calls us.

What we cannot conclude from any of this is that there is no difference between religious music and secular, or that the church should simply adopt every kind of secular style of music in a welcoming spirit. Rather, we have found reasons for some religious music to find a home in the world, and for some of the world's music, when reshaped and transformed, to find a home in church, by the grace of God.

34. Karl Barth, "A Letter of Thanks to Mozart," from the Round Robin in the weekly supplement of the *Luzerner Neuesten Nachrichten*, Jan. 21, 1956; in Karl Barth, *Wolfgang Amadeus Mozart*, trans. Clarence K. Pott (Grand Rapids: William B. Eerdmans, 1986), p. 23.

CHAPTER 7

On Not Giving Short Shrift to the Arts in Liturgy: The Testimony of Pope Benedict XVI (Cardinal Ratzinger)

It has not escaped the notice of students of the arts and liturgy that, when one considers earlier times and compares them with more modern eras, only a relatively small percentage of artists and musicians since the late eighteenth century have produced work for liturgical contexts. In the modern era, churches and other worshiping communities — often facing dwindling financial resources and reduced public influence — have typically lacked the funds and the prestige to compete with secular institutions. In any case, church leaders have not always recognized or fully appreciated what artists and musicians working at their best can offer, if given a chance. Accomplished artists, for their part, have come to relish the greater freedom for innovative and individual expression that they have been afforded by other kinds of supporters and venues, even if that has meant that the very real spiritual and religious roots of their work have sometimes been unrecognized or undernourished.

Given this situation, it is noteworthy when a new pope turns out to be someone whose theological writings as a cardinal included several substantial essays urging the church to respect and encourage the contribution of genuine artistry to the liturgy and rejecting the opinions of those who would give short shrift (so to speak) to the artistry of church architecture and to music's integral role as an art within the liturgy.

In the years when he was Cardinal Joseph Ratzinger, Benedict XVI published those specific arguments, and went on to express a related concern about kinds of art and music that, however popular, might trivialize, or otherwise distract from, the act of worship at its highest. In calling attention to such writings here — above all the document "On the Theological Basis of Church Music,"[1] but also essays collected in *A New Song for the Lord*[2] — I have no wish to engage in debates peculiar to Catholicism, and have no real standing to do so in any case, being Protestant.[3] Nor do I assume that many of those Catholics and Protestants with whom I have a close affinity, theologically, will be inclined to defer readily to the judgments of a pope whose salient opinions in these matters they may associate with a troubling kind of conservativism and elitism. Be that as it may, the reflections of then-Cardinal Ratzinger on the role of art and (especially) music in liturgy warrant serious consideration. In the present context, I will focus exclusively on a cluster of his central arguments and their implications, both positive and negative, and conclude by suggesting (perhaps audaciously) certain ways in which I believe such claims could well be supported, qualified, or extended.

---

1. Pope Benedict XVI (then Cardinal Joseph Ratzinger), "On the Theological Basis of Church Music," in his book *Feast of Faith: Approaches to a Theology of the Liturgy*, trans. Graham Harrison (San Francisco: Ignatius, 1986), pp. 97-126. Subsequent citations of this essay will be made parenthetically in the text.

2. Pope Benedict XVI (then Cardinal Joseph Ratzinger), *A New Song for the Lord: Faith in Christ and Liturgy Today*, trans. Martha M. Matesich (New York: Crossroad, 1996). I am indebted to Anthony Ruff of St. John's School of Theology-Seminary for guiding me to these writings, although my interpretations and conclusions are not necessarily ones he would endorse.

3. For an excellent analysis of significant institutional Catholic documents regarding worship music, see Jan Michael Joncas, *From Sacred Song to Ritual Music: Twentieth-Century Understandings of Roman Catholic Worship Music* (Collegeville, Minn.: Liturgical Press, 1997). See also the essay by Joncas, "An Anniversary Song: Pope John Paul II's 2003 Chirograph for the Centenary of *Tra le Sollecitudini*," in *Music in Christian Worship: At the Service of the Liturgy*, ed. Charlotte Kroeker (Collegeville, Minn.: Liturgical Press, 2005), pp. 47-61. For an extensive discussion of related issues in Christianity more generally, see Frank Burch Brown, *Good Taste, Bad Taste, and Christian Taste: Aesthetics in Religious Life* (New York: Oxford University Press, 2000).

Writing in 1981, Cardinal Ratzinger opened his important essay "On the Theological Basis of Church Music" by expressing his astonishment at a statement found in the German edition of the documents of Vatican II (1962-65). He noted that the (obviously estimable) editors Karl Rahner and Herbert Vorgrimler, when introducing the chapter on sacred music in the Constitution on the Sacred Liturgy *(Sacrosanctum Concilium)*, had made the observation that genuine art, as found in church music, is "of its very nature — which is esoteric in the best sense — hardly to be reconciled with the nature of the liturgy and the basic principle of liturgical reform" (quoted in *Feast of Faith*, p. 97). What Ratzinger as cardinal describes as so astonishing is the contrast between that claim and the fact that, if one turns to the Constitution on the Liturgy itself, one finds the quite different assertion that music is not "merely an addition and ornamentation of the liturgy" but is itself liturgy, and integral to the "complete liturgical action" (quoted in *Feast of Faith*, p. 97).[4]

Of course neither Rahner nor Vorgrimler want to banish all music from worship, Ratzinger says. In his view, what they find alien to the nature of worship is "art music, i.e., the musical heritage of the Western Church." Consequently, when the Council recommends that the "treasury of sacred music is to be preserved and cultivated with great care," these German editors simply, albeit amazingly, deny that this is to be done within the liturgy. And when the Council recommends that choirs should be cultivated "especially in cathedral churches," these same editors imply by their explanatory comments that this should be restricted entirely to cathedral contexts, and even then should never obstruct the people's participation. In Ratzinger's account, the upshot of all this is that Rahner and Vorgrimler do not think of the normal musical component of the liturgy as "actual church music" but as "so-called utility music" (*Feast of Faith*, pp. 97-98). While Ratzinger never fully explains what he supposes that term means, presumably it would

---

4. For the most recent English translation of the "Constitution on the Sacred Liturgy," see *Vatican Council II: Constitutions, Decrees, Declarations*, revised translation in inclusive language, ed. Austin Flannery (Northport, N.Y.: Costello, 1996), pp. 117-61.

be music that moves one through the liturgy in a functionally appropriate way but without exhibiting any developed aesthetic or artistic integrity of its own, lest it might for a moment be enjoyed for its own sake.

By way of critique, Ratzinger points out that what Rahner and Vorgrimler manage to do, in effect, is to dissolve an important and necessary tension present in *Sacrosanctum Concilium*. In his judgment, there should never have been any doubt that the Council document embraces "actual church music." Beyond the points mentioned above, it emphasizes the importance of teaching church music in seminaries and of training church musicians. It speaks of the desirability of establishing "higher institutes of sacred music" and includes, in such music, not only Gregorian chant but also the complex musical art of polyphony. Besides that, Ratzinger says, the document waxes "positively enthusiastic" about the pipe organ, while encouraging other musical instruments as well.

At the same time, however — and here is where the tension enters in — the document also expresses "a desire to see the liturgy completely open to all, a desire for the common participation of all in the liturgical action, including liturgical singing, and this, inevitably, must put a curb on artistic requirements" (*Feast of Faith*, p. 99). This imperative to include everyone is clearly manifest in the now famous call for "full, conscious, and active participation" of the people. And that, inevitably, entails simplification. Thus there is in the document a "tension between the demands of art and the simplicity of the liturgy" (*Feast of Faith*, p. 99). But however that tension is addressed, Ratzinger implies, it is a mistake to accept either the common modernist notion that genuine art must be completely autonomous in every sense, existing only for its own sake, or the correlative notion of many modern liturgists that nothing with the integrity of a real work of art or music has any business being enlisted in the service of the unique and more encompassing "art" of the entire liturgy. There (they have often wrongly assumed) it could only call attention to itself and interrupt the overall integrity of the liturgy.

By ignoring the document's advocacy for a truly artistic — albeit nonetheless suitable — music in liturgy, and embracing only the imperative for the full and complete participation of everyone even in the singing, Rahner and Vorgrimler are in no way exceptional, Ratzinger is quick to admit. On the contrary, they represent the majority interpretation of the Constitution on the Sacred Liturgy as it has been applied in the years following Vatican II. In practice, the document has been read "one-sidedly," so that a rule of thumb has emerged — namely, that what the liturgy needs is utility music. Ratzinger laments, "The years which followed [Vatican II] witnessed the increasingly grim impoverishment which follows when beauty for its own sake is banished from the Church and all is subordinated to the principle of 'utility.' One shudders at the lackluster face of the postconciliar liturgy as it has become, or one is bored with its banality and its lack of artistic standards; all the same, this development has at least created a situation in which one can begin to ask questions" (*Feast of Faith,* p. 100).

According to Ratzinger, those questions have been heightened by two opposing trends in modern culture. On the one hand, modern art and music have become increasingly specialized, abstruse, and alien to the general public. On the other hand, there is among the public at large a craze for the "catchy melody," for sentimental schmaltz, and in church for whatever is "useful" (*Feast of Faith,* p. 101).

And yet, he says, the conflicts and antitheses we witness today are only a contemporary variation of a problem that goes back to the dawn of Christianity (*Feast of Faith,* p. 101). And much of the problem boils down to difficulties the church has experienced from the beginning in attempting to discern how to "spiritualize" culture without abandoning its commitment to the Incarnation and to the meaning of Incarnation for the faith's cultural expression, including arts and music. Part of the challenge, historically, is that the church grew up in the context of a certain sort of Judaism — of a Judaism in which the synagogue rather than the temple came to be central — which meant that Christianity inevitably took on a "more or less puritanical form," in which not only were images off-limits, but musical instruments themselves were set aside (*Feast of Faith,* p. 108), although temple worship had used them extensively. While the church that continued for centuries to forgo instruments affirmed, in due course, the spiritual value of images, many theologians after Vatican II seem to have reversed even that, by advocating an increasingly spare worship space. Ratzinger associates such a retreat from the artistry of the audible and the visual with a disembodied spirituality that, after all, privileges the music of the heart more than music that is heard and forgets about how God can be glorified not only through invisible truth but also through and in the visible image (*Feast of Faith*, p. 110). Again, this bias against the senses is nothing new, he concedes. Venerable theologians such as Augustine and Thomas Aquinas likewise were less than welcoming of a truly embodied spirituality, and the theological bias against sensuous art was exaggerated (as Ratzinger argues in discussing Thomas) by a theology of God's "absolute immutability and impassibility." Inherited from Greek philosophy, this theological emphasis at its extreme was later to create "a barrier to any satisfactory theology, not only of church music, but of all prayer whatever," since it led in time to a thin rationalism that cast a shadow over the theory of liturgy itself (*Feast of Faith*, p. 112).

To all this, Ratzinger juxtaposes the counter-influence of the psalms, which have played such a major part in the life of the church. For the psalms manifest "an utterly unpuritanical delight in music" (*Feast of Faith*, p. 114), a delight in the whole cosmos and the music of creation, and yet express powerful prayers of lamentation and become, also, the voice of the poor. Citing the work of Hans Urs von Balthasar, Ratzinger asserts that such prayerful transformation or indeed "glorification" is "the central reason why Christian liturgy must be cosmic liturgy, why it must as it were orchestrate the mystery of Christ with all the voices of creation" (*Feast of Faith*, p. 115). Whatever theology may say, the fully experienced act of praise in worship is recognized as more than mere understanding, knowing, and doing. "Anyone who has ever experienced the transforming power of great liturgy, great art, great music, will know this," because those things awaken the inner person, the whole being (*Feast of Faith*, p. 116).

When Ratzinger returns more directly to present-day considerations, he makes several moves that may be startling. Because true church music entails not simply the use of ready-made styles but the transformation of music in the Spirit — a transformation "which implies both death and resurrection" — Ratzinger states, "The Church has had to be critical of all ethnic music; it could not be allowed untransformed into the sanctuary" (*Feast of Faith*, p. 118). Thinking partly of the ancient church, he declares that pagan music indulges in an ecstasy of the senses without "elevating the senses into the spirit." This kind of imbalance, he says, "recurs in modern popular music," with the consequence that the music becomes seductive and fails to lead to the true God (*Feast of Faith*, pp. 118-19). More controversially still, he argues that the basic reason why "elements of African pagan music are taken up with such facility into post-Christian pagan music" is that our modern world, for all its superficial differences from the traditional African setting, is in many ways "pagan and primitive." Whereas, if music is to be the medium of genuine worship, it needs "purifying" so that it can be truly "elevating" (*Feast of Faith*, p. 119).

In the Western world, Ratzinger affirms, the music that best embodies the fruits of the struggle to achieve a balance of spirit and body, and in which the "spiritualization of the senses is the true spiritualization of the spirit," is in fact "the great church music of the West — indeed, Western music as a whole," including the music of Palestrina and Mozart. Despite that seeming affirmation of the spirituality of Western art music in general, Ratzinger goes on to stress that the struggle has been long and has produced kinds of music that could never have been foreseen in the beginning (*Feast of Faith*, p. 119). That said, he also insists that liturgical music must be humble. And through the liturgy it must orient itself toward the incarnate Word — though, as even Thomas Aquinas recognized, this does not so much require that the listener be able to hear and understand all the individual words as that the listener understand the music to be for the praise of God (*Feast of Faith*, pp. 120-21).

Rounding out his discussion with a set of basic governing principles (as contrasted with specific rules), Ratzinger first reiterates that liturgy must be for all. And a certain simplicity is needed to accomplish that. But that is very different from yielding to the temptation to be simplistic — manifest in what today we might term "dumbing down." Second, he affirms that there is no reason why the unity of Catholic worship cannot be preserved while allowing considerable diversity in the arts employed, with a cathedral making use of more "ambitious" arts, for example, and employing art at different levels even in the same church, depending on the occasion. Third, while liturgy is to entail the active participation of the whole people, it is unduly constricting to confine the idea of active participation to something merely external. There is a kind of listening, attending, and spiritual participation that is fully active. Moreover, not to put too fine a point on it, there are a good many people, he says, who can sing much better in their hearts than with their mouths, and who do so best when in the presence of those who have the special gift of song. "It is as if they themselves actually sing in the others." He thus, by implication, leaves ample room for the use of choirs and of music more complex than anything within the reach of the average singer in worship. As he had said earlier, this positive image of receptive participation "goes back to a conception of activity, community and equality which . . . knows the unity-creating power of shared listening, shared wonder, the shared experience of being moved at a level deeper than words" (*Feast of Faith*, p. 101).

That leads to the fourth point, which is Ratzinger's claim that the church's mission is higher than can readily be served by "utility music," or music that is merely "comfortable and serviceable at the parish level." The church is to be at once a place where the human "cry of distress is brought to the ear of God" and a place where, in the very process of "humanizing" the world, the church will "arouse the voice of the cosmos and, by glorifying the creator, elicit the glory of the cosmos itself, making it also glorious, beautiful, habitable, and beloved." Indeed, writes Ratzinger in one of the most striking sentences of all, "Next to the saints, the art which the Church has produced is the only real 'apologia' for her history. It is this glory which witnesses to the Lord, not theology's clever explanations for all the terrible things which, lamentably, fill the pages of her history" (*Feast of Faith*, p. 124). In truth, "beauty and love form the true consolation in this world, bringing it as near as possible to the world of the resurrection. The

Church must maintain high standards: she must be a place where beauty can be at home" (*Feast of Faith*, p. 125).

In his fifth and final principle, Ratzinger affirms, with the Constitution on the Liturgy, that in the lands around the world there are many different kinds of music that should be given "proper esteem," even if care must also be exercised that those various indigenous kinds of music, as employed in worship, are used and shaped with sensitivity, as a consequence of which they may be "raised to a higher level" than ever before. The irony, according to Ratzinger, is that interpreters of Vatican II, in reaching out appropriately to other cultures, have become forgetful of so much of Europe's own musical heritage (*Feast of Faith*, p. 125). It is not that those European works of artistic church music should stand as timeless models, any more than the works of great Latin theologians should be regarded as having attained some "ultimate theological perfection." Yet the church cannot afford to lose this rich inheritance, which "developed in her own matrix and yet belongs to the whole of humanity." To preserve and cultivate that heritage of musical art, however, it is essential that the church actually use it to glorify God in the place where it was born — in worship (*Feast of Faith*, p. 126).

It is neither possible nor necessary to examine in detail the several other articles Cardinal Ratzinger produced on church music and related themes, including architecture, prior to his becoming pope. The main points are similar, though tailored to different purposes. Those other essays, however, sometimes introduce a new tone and emphasis. In the 1990 essay "Sing Artistically for God," Cardinal Ratzinger is more emphatic about the extent to which, ever since the nineteenth century, the culture outside the church has appeared farther and farther removed from its religious matrix; meanwhile, to those in the church itself, it has become increasingly obvious "that we are at a loss as to how faith can and should express itself culturally in the present age."[5] He is

5. Pope Benedict XVI (Cardinal Joseph Ratzinger), "Sing Artistically for God," in *A New Song for the Lord*, pp. 119-39. Subsequent citations of this essay will be made parenthetically in the text.

more concerned about the widespread influence of popular music as commercially manufactured, and more adamant that the alternative ideal of beauty for its own sake, which has its value when properly understood, has been perverted in the modernist idea of art for art's sake. That principle is particularly problematical when expressed in avant-garde musical styles impenetrable to everyday listeners and dedicated to no discernible purpose other than a peculiar virtuosity (*A New Song*, pp. 121, 133).

Anchoring his specifically theological reflections in an analysis of the Psalms, Ratzinger argues that the "integral way of humanly expressing joy or sorrow, consent or complaint which occurs in singing [with or without instruments] is necessary for responding to God, who touches us precisely in the totality of our being" (*A New Song*, p. 126). Because of the need to sing, however, the faithful also need to create culture, and "not just carry it along like a piece of clothing" (*A New Song*, p. 127). This, in turn, requires singing a new song — and singing old songs anew. This is not just singing of any sort, but singing artistically. It means employing art as a kind of wisdom that is in tune with the Word — and producing art that is "high" in the sense of participating in God's own creativity, rather than making something aesthetic that is valued completely as one's own invention, as can happen in elitist art (*A New Song*, p. 129).

But if an aesthetic elitism that distorts the creative process is a problem for liturgy, so is pastoral pragmatism, which in Ratzinger's analysis is only looking out for success (*A New Song*, p. 134). Having again made this point, however, Ratzinger interrupts himself to allude to an issue raised in an earlier lecture, published in 1986 as "The Image of the World and of Human Beings in the Liturgy and Its Expression in Church Music."[6] As Ratzinger explains, and as one can read for oneself, what was most controversial about that essay, with respect to music, had been its condemnation of rock music, which Ratzinger de-

---

6. Pope Benedict XVI (Cardinal Joseph Ratzinger), "The Image of the World and of Human Beings in the Liturgy and Its Expression in Church Music," in *A New Song for the Lord*, pp. 141-63. Subsequent citations of this essay will be made parenthetically in the text.

scribed as reviving the ancient Dionysian drive toward stupor and ecstasy, but as connecting that drive with drugs and an illusion of redemption through total uninhibitedness and irresponsibility (*A New Song*, pp. 155-56). In the context of the later essay on singing artistically for God, Ratzinger acknowledges that his earlier condemnation of rock music generated a storm of protest (which is not surprising, in view of the sweeping nature of the critique and the fact that it went far beyond questions of liturgical appropriateness). He declares, however, that he has heard no persuasive counterarguments, and proceeds to consider the phenomenon not of rock itself but of the kind of commercial pop that has widely invaded the liturgy. Unlike genuine folk music, he says, commercial pop music has little connection with communities and real-life experience. It is part of a mass, artificial culture that is "geared to quantity, production, and success," a "culture of the measurable and marketable" (*A New Song*, p. 135).

It is not difficult to see where Cardinal Ratzinger's soul is at home, artistically and culturally. That becomes evident once more in a last essay, "In the Presence of the Angels I Will Sing Your Praise," based on an address he gave in 1992 at Regensburg Cathedral upon the departure of his brother from the post of cathedral choirmaster.[7] One of the most notable features of this essay is Ratzinger's resounding affirmation of the idea that, even after Vatican II, the choir can serve a distinctive yet representative function. It can sing out in the *Sanctus*, for example, singing on behalf of the people, or indeed as the voice of the people, and not sound as though it is merely performing in a concert (*A New Song*, pp. 180-82). In this way the choir can draw the congregation "into cosmic praise and into the open expanse of heaven and earth more powerfully than its own stammering" (*A New Song*, p. 180).

In reflecting briefly on the implications and possible limitations of the theology of music, art, and liturgy that Ratzinger sets forth in these

7. Pope Benedict XVI (Cardinal Joseph Ratzinger), "'In the Presence of the Angels I Will Sing Your Praise': The Regensburg Tradition and the Reform of the Liturgy," in *A New Song for the Lord*, pp. 164-87. Subsequent citations of this essay will be made parenthetically in the text.

rich and provocative essays, one can hardly overlook the relevance of his discussions to controversies and practices in worship and the arts well beyond the sphere of Roman Catholicism. Moreover, it would be hard to find a theologian who makes a more passionate defense of "high" forms of art and music as potentially something called for by the high calling of the liturgy itself.

There is no denying that Ratzinger's primary arguments tend to go against the grain of much modern liturgical reform in Protestant and Catholic circles, which has insisted on the nearly absolute priority of accessibility in "ritual" art and music, and on the active and overt participation of everyone in the liturgy. Ratzinger challenges those assumptions and suggests that a great many churches and their leaders have acted prematurely in setting aside the vast majority of previously treasured and potentially rewarding works of artistic church music (for example). From a North American perspective, one can corroborate that, for a variety of reasons — in attending not only to market forces but also to legitimate ethical and pastoral imperatives to be more inclusive and egalitarian — church leaders appear to have been all too eager to treat some of the more demanding yet potentially exalting arts as simply irrelevant. Indeed, some have rushed to label those arts as inherently inappropriate, elitist, or irreverent, under the simple pretext that liturgy is the work of the people — a skewed etymology, one might note, since "liturgy" from its start in Greek has always referred to a public work that can be done for, by, or on behalf of the people in general.

What Ratzinger prompts us to examine more deeply is the possibility that long traditions of highly (if generally humbly) wrought music and art did, in their time and over time, become at once beautiful, expressive, and powerfully artistic works; and yet, in their very way of being artistic, those kinds of art and music became integral to liturgical purposes of the highest sort. Indeed, they may have become truly liturgical, in the highest sense, in ways that other works and styles, frequently today bought off the shelves of commercial music supermarkets, are very unlikely to be.

Ratzinger's call for retaining, reviving, and creating works of art and music that are engaging and transformative of the whole being, and in keeping with the highest needs of both body and spirit, is worth pondering. In that case we should also avoid a dichotomy that some have created by arguing that in liturgy it must be the singing rather than the song, and the music-making rather than the music itself, that leads believers "into the mystery."[8] That may very well be true as a description of the primary focus in worship, experientially or "phenomenologically" speaking. And it is true of more improvisatory and process-oriented kinds of music-making from various indigenous and popular traditions worldwide, which have often not been fully appreciated. But when it comes to musical "works" by gifted composers as such, it is clearly both the song and the singing, both the musical composition and the music-making, that lead believers "into the mystery." To minimize the role of the former in enabling the latter creates the false impression that the church can easily dispense with artistic musical compositions and lose nothing in the process.

Moreover, Ratzinger makes a strong case against any glib dismissal of certain kinds of music or art just because they are presented by a choir or some other artistically trained group, as though that would inevitably entail mere entertainment or sheer performance. Taking this line of thought one step further, one could argue that, while some ways of presenting music in church are indeed objectionably performance-oriented, that does not mean that ways of "performing" cannot be found that invite and evoke more participative listening and viewing on the part of all those assembled in worship. Although Ratzinger himself never says so, this might apply not only to the choral presentation of Western "classical" music in worship but also to certain styles of gospel music — styles that, especially in African-American traditions, feature a gospel choir or possibly a "praise band" whose musi-

---

8. See Edward Foley, *Ritual Music: Studies in Liturgical Musicology* (Beltsville, Md.: Pastoral Press, 1995), p. 139, where — in a book otherwise full of valuable insights — Foley may exhibit a tendency to overemphasize the communal and functional side of liturgical (or, as he prefers, "ritual") music, perhaps overcompensating for a historical tendency of the church to speak of sacred music in purely objective and impersonal terms.

cal offering and initiative are acknowledged and answered by the gathered assembly, audibly and in movement.[9]

We could also say, however, that the capacity to listen actively and in a truly spiritual dimension, especially to music that is from a tradition that is unfamiliar or even alien, is something that requires careful cultivation — more so than Ratzinger himself seems to acknowledge.[10] And it is a capacity that people at home with the Western classical artistic and musical traditions beloved by Ratzinger must themselves acquire when encountering traditions very different in stylistic vocabulary — more exuberant styles, perhaps, or overtly animated, or intentionally entrancing.

Like most people, Ratzinger is strongest and most persuasive in what he affirms. He is less persuasive — and at times offensive — in what he rejects and condemns. His blanket condemnation of mass culture and pop music, while not without some basis, shows little attempt to take into account the wide range of what is possible in popular idioms. Nor does it show any awareness of the many recent critiques of just such sweeping dismissals of mass culture (dismissals that were once common among Marxists, incidentally). And while in the later essays he becomes more deft at dealing with worldwide and ethnic cultures, he still seems only vaguely conscious of contextual factors and unaware of how difficult it is to make definite cross-cultural judgments of the sort that he attempts periodically — never considering, for instance, that in more rhythmic and repetitive music (even when "pagan") there could at times be something more at work than mind-numbing self-obliteration. Likewise, he is evidently inclined to think of what some might call the objective qualities of the music as such without also considering the manner in which the music may be presented and the subjective differences in how it is likely to be received in particular communities. In that way, Ratzinger is relatively insensitive to

9. See Melva Wilson Costen, *In Spirit and in Truth: The Music of African-American Worship* (Louisville: Westminster John Knox, 2004).

10. For an extensive discussion of such issues in liturgical music — albeit with a functional and social emphasis that Ratzinger might find extreme — see Foley, *Ritual Music*.

ways in which diverse cultures may, over time, find their own distinctive styles of music and art suitable to an incarnational spirituality and to the glorification of God.

Despite these and other limitations, Ratzinger rightly challenges to the core any assumption that the arts used in liturgy should, in effect, be nothing more than self-effacing, interchangeable parts, or that notably artistic musical works and styles long shaped to the ends of liturgy could be rendered mute without a high cost to the liturgy itself. Equally important, he undercuts any temptation to suppose that it is somehow un-Christian to seek out musical and artistic forms that are exceptionally powerful and beautiful — artistic forms that, by the grace of God, can give appropriate shape and voice to the highest purposes of the liturgy.

CHAPTER 8

On Being Beautiful and
Religious at the Same Time:
Reviving Plotinus

Beautifully Religious

In today's world, to speak of being beautiful is almost immediately to conjure up the image of someone's physical beauty, most often a woman's. Yet we all acknowledge that there are many other kinds of beauty. It is not unusual to hear worshipers comment on the beauty of a particular service, such as a church wedding or an Easter vigil. Indeed, in the year 987, ambassadors of Prince Vladimir of Kiev, who in reporting back to the prince commended Byzantine Christianity as the best choice for the still-pagan Russian people, did so partly on the basis of the beauty of its worship and art. After visiting the great church of Hagia Sophia in Byzantium, they are said to have declared, "We knew not whether we were in heaven or on earth. For on earth there is no such splendor or such beauty, and we are at a loss to describe it. We know only that God dwells there among men, and their service is fairer than the ceremonies of other nations. For we cannot forget that beauty."[1]

When it comes to worship and its physical setting, however, Protestants (and Calvinists in particular) have tended to be suspicious of

---

1. *Russian Primary Chronicle*, quoted in Thomas F. Mathews, *Byzantium: From Antiquity to the Renaissance* (New York: Harry N. Abrams–Perspectives, 1998), p. 98.

richly sensuous or elaborate worship ceremonies and of overtly beautiful or ornate buildings, which they have often judged to be ostentatious, wasteful, or superficial. Americans in large community churches
(often prospering financially) often pay scant attention to beauty of
built form, preferring to use strictly utilitarian multimedia worship
halls. And the Catholic Church itself, which can be exuberant and un-
restrained in church architecture such as Mexican baroque or Bavar-
ian rococco — and which is often remarkably sensuous in its festivals
and liturgies, whether in Prague or in Lima, Peru — also has a strong
ascetic streak. This emerges not only in various monastic traditions, as
one would expect, but also in liturgical reform. Even the influential
post–Vatican II document *Environment and Art in Catholic Worship*
repeatedly emphasizes "the virtue of simplicity and commonness in liturgical texts, gestures, music, etc.," despite making a point of confess-
ing that too often the liturgy of the church "has suffered historically
from a kind of minimalism and an overriding concern for efficiency."[2]
Alternatively, though many an Eastern Orthodox theologian would
join with the nineteenth-century Russian novelist Dostoyevsky in affirming that beauty can and will ultimately save the world, it is not always clear just what is meant by "beauty" of that sort, and the extent
to which its redemptive work takes a genuinely sensory, let alone
worldly, form. Some Lutherans (among others) who embrace a theology of the cross would want to ask, Doesn't the Crucifixion mean a
kind of divine self-emptying or *kenosis* that loses all concern for out-
ward beauty in the process?

Accordingly, even in a time when theologies of beauty abound,[3]

2. National Conference of Catholic Bishops and Bishops' Committee on the Liturgy,
Environment and Art in Catholic Worship (United States Catholic Conference, 1993),
paragraphs 17 and 14.

3. For examples of the more recent theologies of beauty, see Richard Viladesau,
Theological Aesthetics: God in Imagination, Beauty, and Art (New York: Oxford University Press, 1999); Richard Harries, *Art and the Beauty of God: A Christian Understanding* (New York: Mowbray, 1993); Patrick Sherry, *Spirit and Beauty,* 2d ed. (London: SCM Press, 2002); Edward Farley, *Faith and Beauty: A Theological Aesthetic*
(Burlington, Vt.: Ashgate, 2001); Alejandro García-Rivera, *The Community of the*

anyone contemplating the conjunction of beauty and worship is likely to confront, sooner or later, the awkward question of what sort of beauty to seek in worship, and whether a truly "spiritual worship" can afford to make much of beauty that is visible, audible, sensory, palpable. To what extent are beauty and spirituality compatible? Under what conditions is the beauty of a person (however saintly), or of artistry, to be perceived as religious or as integral to its value in worship? Can the beauty of something (whether a person or a liturgy) ever *contribute* to its being religious or worshipful? How one answers such questions has everything to do with the role one hopes or expects artistry to play in worship and in religious life. That is because, whatever else we may mean by "art" in the aesthetic sense, we are usually talking about something that engages the senses and whose beauty or expressiveness is to some significant extent *embodied* in particular perceptible forms and not only imagined or known abstractly.

For most of us it is a long way from thinking about beauty in the context of present-day worship or culture to pondering ancient philosophy. But countless generations of devout Christians and theologians up to the present day — whether Protestant or Catholic — have been indebted directly or indirectly to ancient philosophers such as Plato and Plotinus. Indeed, the third-century pagan philosopher Plotinus offered a whole system of thought that connected beauty with spirituality, and did so in ways that — especially as transmitted through Augustine — were to have a profound influence on Christian theology, including the practical theology of John Calvin. To revisit Plotinus and see how his philosophy of beauty and spirituality might be "converted" or re-formed — much as we did with Calvin himself in relation to music — will thus give us an opportunity to reshape some of the very foundational thinking employed or assumed by Christians when reflecting on beauty and on the sensuous and artistic dimensions of worship and the Christian life.

Beautiful (Collegeville, Minn.: Michael Glazer/Liturgical Press, 1999); and David Bentley Hart, *The Beauty of the Infinite: The Aesthetics of Christian Truth* (Grand Rapids: William B. Eerdmans, 2003).

The legacy of Plotinus is mixed, having played into a dualism of matter versus spirit that he only partly embraced. And the more positive spiritual sense of beauty and art that Plotinus describes is, unfortunately, rather difficult to retrieve, both because of the quite different assumptions that are predominant in modern life and because of tensions and inconsistencies within Plotinus's own thought. Fortunately, a recent book by Margaret Miles is available to assist us. In her study *Plotinus on Body and Beauty*, Miles seeks in part to recover Plotinus for the present, just as we do.[4] One way in which she tries to accomplish that is by showing how, from Plotinus's point of view, "the beautiful life is made beautiful by light from its [spiritual] source" (*Plotinus,* p. 158). Life is not the only thing, however, that Plotinus thinks is spiritually enlightened through beauty. The same is true of art and, to some extent, of anything that so much as exists. That is because, from the perspective offered by Plotinus, beauty is intrinsic to existence, goodness, and spirituality. Viewed in terms of what we might anachronistically call "aesthetics" (a term coined in the eighteenth century), the goal of everything is to attain its proper level of beauty, and to contribute its beauty to the greater whole.

But if that is so, and if Miles is right in thinking that we can learn from such thinking in the present day, we need to pose some questions right away. What are we supposed to think of when we say "beauty"? Does beauty come in degrees and kinds? What are we to make of bodily beauty, or the beauty of art (and, by extension, of worship)? How do we learn to discern beauty at all and to discriminate higher forms of beauty from lower? Furthermore, if beauty is an integral part of the highest vision of the spiritual life (and, by implication, worship), what kind of beauty best serves that purpose?

Such questions have an ethical dimension (in the Greek sense of being germane to a good life). Here, however, I will mainly treat them from the standpoint of theological aesthetics, although in relation to

4. Margaret R. Miles, *Plotinus on Body and Beauty: Society, Philosophy, and Religion in Third-Century Rome* (Malden, Mass.: Blackwell, 1999). The quotation is Miles's paraphrase of Plotinus. Subsequent citations of this volume will be made parenthetically in the text.

ethics. My goal, in the end, is not to analyze all the finer points of Plotinus's thought but to use Miles's treatment of Plotinus as a way of grappling with one central issue we have already identified: imagining how human beings and their works of art, and artful worship, can be beautiful and religious at the same time. While I make no attempt to spell out all the implications this has for liturgical aesthetics, I am intending to help provide fundamental reasons, from an aesthetic standpoint, for a new emphasis on beauty within an embodied spirituality that includes the life of worship in a central way.

Beauty: An Overview

Before we look more closely at features of Plotinus's view of beauty that Margaret Miles finds especially salient, we would do well to step back and consider briefly how beauty has figured in Western theology and spirituality.[5] Rarely the primary focus of theology and spirituality, beauty nonetheless plays a part in both. From Clement of Alexandria (c. 150-c. 215) and Augustine (354-430), through Bonaventure (c. 1217-1274) and Thomas Aquinas (c. 1225-1274), to Hans Urs von Balthasar (1905-1988) and Paul Evdokimov (1901-1970), theologians of various kinds have held that beauty finds its ultimate source and final perfection in God. All created beauty, they have said, reflects and participates to some degree, at least by analogy, in beauty that is divine. The higher forms of beauty, moreover, can attune the soul spiritually and morally. To be remade in the image of Christ is thus, as Eastern Orthodox theologians have affirmed, to be transformed in and by genuinely Christ-filled beauty.

The main inspiration for such views in antiquity was not, to begin with, overtly Christian philosophy. It was the philosophy of Plato (c. 428–c. 348 B.C.) as reinterpreted through the Neoplatonism of

---

5. In what follows, I have borrowed and paraphrased brief passages from my article "Beauty" in the *New Westminster Dictionary of Christian Spirituality*, ed. Philip Sheldrake (Louisville: Westminster John Knox, 2005), pp. 145-46.

Plotinus (c. 205-270) and the Christian mysticism of Dionysius the Pseudo-Areopagite (c. 500). Medieval scholastics also drew on Aristotle (384-322 B.C.) when a number of them framed the idea that beauty — along with goodness, truth, and unity — is a "transcendental" property of being, so that, to the extent that something exists, it is in some measure beautiful.

In all of this, the idea of beauty itself was never extremely precise or entirely stable. For the ancient Greeks, beauty *(kalon)* had to do not only with aesthetics in our sense but also with goodness. It is that which lures our desire and admiration and which, it was generally agreed, pleases through proportion and symmetry. Since proportion can be expressed numerically, beauty also has a distinctly mathematical and rational dimension.

Medieval ideas of beauty *(formositas)* retained an intellectual and spiritual tenor while placing particular emphasis on delight. In the eyes of scholastic philosophers, culminating in Thomas Aquinas, beauty consists in harmonious proportion, integrity, and radiance or "splendor" of form. At the same time, beauty gives delight in the very act of its being perceived. In approaching the Bible, which says little about beauty as such, theologians paid particular attention to Wisdom 11:21, which stresses the rational aspect of creativity by declaring that God made all things according to "measure and number and weight."

Both the Neoplatonic and the scholastic traditions had a less rational side as well — one that, far from hurrying past sensible beauty, sought to glory in it appropriately. This sometimes led to a broadly sacramental approach to such arts as church architecture, stained glass, and manuscript illumination.

By the eighteenth century, however, when the idea of the "fine arts" took hold in Europe, beauty was increasingly understood in subjective terms. While Immanuel Kant (1724-1804) could still regard beauty as a symbol of the morally good, beauty in much modern philosophy became essentially set free from any necessary grounding in reality and was divorced from any inherent connection to morality.

Much of the resulting ambiguity concerning the ethical and religious meaning of artistry and beauty remains to this day. Art, for instance, is widely seen as essentially self-contained and self-expressive, free of moral obligations, and yet it is also frequently understood as engaging at least indirectly in social critique or even as something profoundly prophetic, and quite often as revelatory of insights that cannot be expressed in ordinary words. That kind of tension in thinking about the character and purpose of art has affected the whole enterprise of theological aesthetics. Thus, even though recently there has been a major revival of theological interest in aesthetics, as I have noted, the arts are often marginalized in such work. This is perhaps done out of hesitation to enter into a realm in which many theologians feel lacking in expertise. But art may also be neglected, theologically, out of habits formed centuries earlier, when art's very association with the senses, excessive emotion, and unfettered imagination aroused theological suspicions.[6] In any case, there is no consensus, by and large, as to what place beauty — and artistic beauty in particular — can and should play in theology, in the morally good life, or in religious practice and worship.

What Would Plotinus Say?

In the chapter that concludes *Plotinus on Body and Beauty,* Margaret Miles ventures to present us with "Plotinus for the Present." Along with expressing certain reservations and criticisms, she commends aspects of what Plotinus has to say about body and its relationship to soul, and likewise his ideas of the sensible world (the world perceptible to the senses) and its relation to what Plotinus called "intellect" (akin to Plato's realm of ideas, but not a separate sphere of reality as it was in Plato). Miles then goes on to talk about Plotinus's thought in

6. Hans Urs von Balthasar's major work in theological aesthetics gives relatively little attention to the arts: see *The Glory of the Lord: A Theological Aesthetics,* 7 vols., various translators (San Francisco: Ignatius Press, 1982-89). The same is true of David Bentley Hart's *The Beauty of the Infinite,* of Patrick Sherry's *Spirit and Beauty,* and of Edward Farley's *Faith and Beauty: A Theological Aesthetic* — all of which make substantial contributions in other respects.

relation to questions of moral engagement and the concerns of feminism. Beauty is hardly mentioned in any of this. But in the context of depicting the worldview of Plotinus as a non-dogmatic kind of religion (albeit without ritual or an actual worshiping community), Miles highlights two interrelated "spiritual disciplines" that involve beauty: first, the discipline of contemplating and imagining the real, which includes a receptive (but not passive) perception of beauty; and second, the discipline of attentiveness to beauty as the mark "of the presence of the One, the great beauty" (*Plotinus,* p. 178). Last, Miles connects beauty with mutual communal responsibility, as something implicit in "Plotinus's description of the connectedness of living things in a vast, interdependent, and beautiful universe" (*Plotinus,* p. 180). This beautifully intimate interconnectedness is not evident, she says, to the "sluggish eye," but comes as a result of "spiritual discipline" (*Plotinus,* p. 182).

Anyone who has read Miles's discussion leading up to her final chapter will realize that she is selective in choosing what of Plotinus she will recommend as especially pertinent today. Furthermore, throughout her study, Miles is judicious in distilling in a lucid way the bewildering complexity of the *Enneads* (the sole extant work of Plotinus). There is no need in the present context to unpack her discussion in detail. Nor will we want to venture too far, on our own, into the vast complexities of Plotinus and his metaphysics. But I will fill out and modify Miles's picture to some extent as I relate Plotinus's thought to our central question of how being beautiful is, or can be, related to being religious, and indirectly to the place of beautiful art in worship.

Body and Soul

Miles knows she faces a challenge in trying to expound the relevance of a philosopher whose life the ancient biographer (and former student of Plotinus), Porphyry, chose to introduce by saying, "Plotinus, the philosopher our contemporary, seemed ashamed of being in the body."[7] No matter that Porphyry himself would have regarded his remark as a thinly veiled compliment. No matter, either, that a good many philosophers of that era, in a variety of schools, would have applauded such asceticism. That kind of "praise" would put off most readers today, the majority of whom have tried any number of measures to enhance their body image so as to have no need to be ashamed of being in their particular bodies.

Accordingly, from the very start, Miles emphasizes the complexity of Plotinus's attitudes, and she laments the tendency of most philosophers, from Porphyry to the present, to depict Plotinus as more dualistic than he really was. Yes, she admits, Plotinus does sometimes refer to body as something low and "muddy." He can be found saying that a person with self-control will not keep company with bodily pleasures. He is not beyond arguing that greatness of soul entails despising the sensible things here on earth (*Plotinus*, p. 40). Plotinus in some of his most memorable and eloquent passages urges those who seek wisdom and happiness to flee from the sensory and bodily world to the realm of intellect and of potentially disembodied soul — and, ultimately, to the divine One that transcends everything finite and temporal (*Plotinus*, p. 41; cf. *Enneads* 6 and 7, which emphatically deny any intrinsic role to be played by bodily vision in the spiritual pursuit of the inner vision of "inaccessible beauty").

Miles observes, moreover, that Plotinus had little reason, personally, to take pleasure and pride in being an embodied soul. He lived in a time of horrid plagues, widespread hunger, and brutal gladiator shows. Eventually he himself fell mortally ill with a foul disease that has since been identified as, in all likelihood, leprosy. One can hardly begrudge Plotinus the comfort of his belief that, as Miles puts it, "at body's demise life departs, ready to form and inform other bodies or, ultimately, to retire to union with the universe" (*Plotinus*, p. 25).

---

7. Porphyry, "On the Life of Plotinus and the Arrangement of His Work," in *Plotinus: The Enneads*, 4th ed., trans. Stephen MacKenna (New York: Random House/ Pantheon, 1969), p. 1. For the most part I will rely on the translations of Plotinus that Miles herself provides, but will turn to MacKenna (and Tatarkiewicz below) for supplementary material, making subsequent citations parenthetically in the text.

In thinking specifically of Plotinus for today, we may actually find something refreshing about his treating body as dependent on soul for its genuine beauty. Even in a society that caters to bodily pleasures, we can safely surmise that words releasing us from enslavement to our bodies as such could sound especially appealing to the many baby boomers whose own aging process and bodily vulnerability can no longer be ignored or completely disguised. Be that as it may, aversion to the body as such is not something popular in our time or something Miles herself cares to promote. Accordingly, Miles goes to great lengths to assure her contemporary readers that Plotinus rejects severe asceticism. His is a universe of emanations from the indescribable and invisible One, proceeding to intellect (or Ideas) and, through intellect, to the common soul of all (in which all souls participate and are ultimately unified). Soul in turn creates the plurality of bodies from the forms it receives from intellect. Everything that exists has a share in beauty that derives ultimately from the primal, divine source. Plotinus in this way takes note of the "primary [though not primal] beauty of bodies" (*Plotinus,* p. 41). He shows us, as well, that the world of sense perceptions that is generated by the overflow of the One through intellect is by no means valueless:

> Intellect is, certainly, beautiful, and the most beautiful of all; its place is in pure light and pure radiance and it includes the nature of real beings; this beautiful universe of ours is a shadow and image of it; and it [i.e., intellect] has its place in all glory, because there is nothing unintelligent or dark or unmeasured in it, and it lives a blessed life; so wonder would possess the one who saw this too, and as he should, entered it and became one with it. (*Enneads* 3.8.11, trans. Miles, *Plotinus,* p. 140)

So it is that intellect, which derives its supreme beauty from the invisible One, transmits something of that beauty to the sensible world, which in varying degrees bears its imprint, its image — or appears as its shadow. Furthermore, it is not as though there is really a vast distance between the shadowy reality of sensible beauty and the beauty of intellect or even the ineffable unity of the Good — the One. We should not think of the sensible world and intellect as two separate worlds, but as one world apprehended on two different but intimately related levels, and in two different ways (*Plotinus*, p. 148). Soul mediates between bodily sense and intellect. Because of this intimate relation or mediation, one need not leave one's body to go beyond the body. One can, instead, delve inward in contemplation in order to attain a "vision" of the higher and more beautiful realities.

Plotinus even avers that there is some spiritual advantage to soul in having communication with body, and in thus comparing, as he says, "things which are, in a way, opposite," which also means "learning, in a way more clearly, the better things. For the experience of evil is a clearer knowledge of the Good for those whose power is too weak to know evil with clear intellectual certainty before experiencing it" (4.8.7, trans. Miles, *Plotinus*, p. 71). Miles declares that this is "Plotinus's most forceful argument for the value of soul's descent." Plotinus, she says, "posits a clear hierarchy, but one that gives their full value to both intellect and the senses" (*Plotinus*, p. 71).

Here we must pause. One sees the basis for Miles's first assertion, since Plotinus is indeed forceful here and does argue for the value of soul's communication with body. Her second assertion, however, may seem to overstate the case by claiming that Plotinus gives both intellect and the senses "full value." My own view, as I will explain, is that, while Plotinus gives some important clues as to how we might give "full value" to both intellect and the senses, he does not entirely achieve that balance himself. (Nor, we might add, does his admirer Augustine, or many another Christian theologian over the course of history.) Unfortunately, this very failure to attain a balanced appreciation of the senses in relation to soul and intellect (or mind, *nous*) has contributed to an otherwise perplexing theological neglect of what we today think of as the arts and artistry. A less-than-balanced appraisal of embodied beauty also can make it more difficult to see how beautiful bodies, artworks, and natural objects can be seen as religious by virtue of their beauty, and by implication as being of religious value (in worship or in life) precisely because of that beauty.

Miles, then, does us a service by challenging those who would dismiss Plotinus as a mere dualist who disdains the body and the world of the senses as unworthy of attention. I am suggesting, however, that we need to go further. There are ways to be relatively true to Plotinus while paying greater respect than he normally did to the potential of both body and art to engage and illumine soul.

Being Sensible about Bodily Beauty

Miles is quite right, I think, to insist that, in Plotinus, body and soul are on intimate terms. There is no Manichaean opposition between spirit and body at work here. When on one occasion Plotinus mentions the beauty of Helen of Troy and of "all those women like in loveliness to Aphrodite," it is not by any means to deprecate their bodily beauty. It is, instead, to say that such beauty truly derives not from "material extension" but from the intellectual creating principle and the ideal form that enters through the eyes — a form apprehended as idea and not as mass with magnitude and measure (5.8.2, trans. MacKenna, *Plotinus*). But the very passage that Miles cites above as "Plotinus's most forceful argument for the value of soul's descent" is symptomatic of a pervasive, or at least intermittent, problem in Plotinus's own approach. Here Plotinus comes precariously close to undercutting any genuinely positive attitude toward the "sensible."

To be sure, in the preceding section (4.8.6, trans. MacKenna, *Plotinus*) Plotinus sounds remarkably affirmative about the realm of the many sensory things: sensibles. He insists that there must be something besides the sheer unity of the One, because otherwise the whole of reality would be amorphous. A plurality of some sort is needed — not only the plurality of the ideas and thus of intellect but also (in some fashion) a plurality of souls and "varied forms of sense." All this results from the "inexhaustible power" by which the One — the Good — spontaneously overflows and continuously gives "its gift to the universe, no part of which it can endure to see without some share in its being." Matter itself can never exist apart from its participation in being, nor can it fall outside the "reach of the principle to whose grace it owes its existence" (4.8.6., trans. MacKenna). Plotinus goes on to say, "The loveliness that is in the sense-realm is an index of the nobleness of the Intellectual sphere, displaying its power and its goodness alike; and all things are for ever linked" (4.8.6, trans. MacKenna).

Here we have a warm, almost effusive embrace of sensible reality. It seems very much in keeping with Plotinus's assertion elsewhere that "if the divine did not exist, the transcendently beautiful, in a beauty beyond all thought, what could be lovelier than the things we see? Certainly no reproach can rightly be brought against this world save only that it is not That" (5.8.8, trans. MacKenna, *Plotinus*).

Plotinus, however, does not stop with these passages that are so redolent with the glories of sensible beauty. In the passage to which we referred above, and which Miles quotes at some length (4.8.7), Plotinus states at once that it would be better for soul to dwell in the realm of intellect. Given its "proper nature," soul is presently under compulsion also to participate in the sense realm. Soul when it is embodied need not grieve at not being the highest, through and through, or at occupying a middle rank between pure intellect and sense. Yet, Plotinus says, soul must guard against plunging into the sensory realm with excessive zeal. Soul can put to good use what it sees and suffers here. That, however, is just because soul can compare the highest things with those here, "which are, in a way, opposite," and can attain a better knowledge of the Good by the "experience of evil." In short, the value of the sensible, bodily realm is described, in this passage, as primarily negative, linked more closely with evil than with good. "Here" in everyday reality we encounter what is, "in a way, opposite" of higher reality; we encounter in the sensible realm what amounts to evil.

Elsewhere Plotinus sounds simply neutral regarding the sensible realm and bodily existence. He assures us that, finally, nothing bodily can harm the rightly ordered soul — neither disease nor natural calamity nor the loss of a spouse nor death itself. Whatever happens in the realm of the senses, the rightly disciplined self can attain perfect felicity and can learn to remain calm in the midst of bodily suffering — something many a Stoic or Buddhist of that same era might likewise

aver (1.4.4-8). We are not constituted by our physical life, Plotinus declares (1.4.9). The act of authentic existence entails activity of intellect
that "has no touch whatever with things of sense." Of course we act
upon material things, and they act upon our bodies. But the principle
of intellect that is active in the life of soul "antedates sensation or any
perception" (1.4.9-10, trans. MacKenna, *Plotinus*). What body adds is
material for imagination; like a mirror, imagination that works with
the senses reflects dimly what is good and true. The one who is spiritually adept, however, has no need of life thus "spilled out in sensation"
(1.4.10, trans. MacKenna).

What are we to make of all this? From the perspective offered by
Plotinus, whatever beauty is shown forth by body and sense derives
from soul. Soul, however, does not learn anything new about beauty
from body, though it recognizes bodily beauty and can thereby be reminded of beauty that is invisible. Our souls (ultimately a unity) can,
to be sure, benefit in a limited way from embodiment in the sensible
realm. We can attain a more vivid sense of the Good from encountering evil in the sensible world. But when Plotinus recommends a
method by which to attain a vision of true beauty, he rarely if ever recommends beginning with a close and attentive appreciation of the
beauty of bodies and sensible things, as many would say Plato does in
the *Symposium*. The path toward higher spiritual wisdom, in every
one of Plotinus's accounts, so far as I can tell, entails turning quickly
away from the senses: "How then can you see the sort of beauty a
good soul has? Go back into yourself and look; and if you do not yet
see yourself beautiful, then, just as someone making a statue which has
to be beautiful cuts away here and polishes there, . . . so you too must
cut away excess and straighten the crooked and clear the dark and
make it bright . . . till the divine glory of virtue shines out on you"
(1.6.9, trans. Miles, *Plotinus*). The physical act of sculpting in this case
is merely an analogy, not an instance of a spiritual exercise. We must
develop a spiritual eye that can see what is "beyond all measure and
superior to all quantity"; for no one "ever saw the sun without becoming sun-like. . . . You must first become all god-like and all beautiful if
you intend to see God and beauty" (1.6.9, trans. Miles). Eternal, un-

changing beauty is the goal, perceived through a certain kind of vision, an intellectual vision. We can be certain that the "eye" capable of seeing in a god-like way is not, at this stage, a physical eye. For this eye must see what is beyond all measure and quantity — intellectual beauty and, ultimately, the radiant unity of divine beauty itself. By comparison, the beauty of bodies and natural objects pales almost (never completely) to insignificance.

Art as a Spiritual Sight

The language and concepts of Plotinus are sufficiently different from what most modern Westerners are familiar with that they can sound strange and at times opaque. But they have affinities with forms of mystic philosophy found in Asian thought, such as those originating on the Indian subcontinent (certain Buddhist and Hindu philosophies). And some of Plotinus's concepts entered into Christian thought in powerfully persistent ways, as I have already indicated. It is now time to examine where art fits into the picture.

Plotinus seldom discusses art except by way of analogy with something else. But his statements about art (especially the plastic arts, but also music) are revealing. The ancients had no unified concept of the fine arts (the arts of the beautiful) as that idea came to be developed in eighteenth-century Europe. But much that Plotinus refers to as artistic we would also treat as such. And it is highly pertinent to our topic when Plotinus writes, "I think . . . that those ancient sages, who sought to secure the presence of divine beings by the erection of shrines and statues, showed insight into the nature of the All; they perceived that, though this Soul is everywhere tractable, its presence will be secured all the more readily when an appropriate receptacle is elaborated, a place especially capable of receiving some portion or phase of it, something reproducing it, or representing it and serving like a mirror to catch an image of it" (1.3.11, trans. MacKenna, *Plotinus*). Plotinus does not develop this line of thought further, however, leaving only the hint that the temple and possibly its inevitable sculptures are designed to represent and mirror some aspect of the All-Soul especially well, and should be valued for that reason. Is it because of their beauty that they attract and manifest divinity, or is it because they somehow produce a semblance of a reality that is itself invisible?

In this passage Plotinus says nothing explicit about the beauty of the temple architecture. Hundreds of years before his time, in fact, the classical Greeks were disinclined to see beauty as a defining or omnipresent trait of art. Plotinus is perhaps the first philosopher to think of all art as beautiful by design and definition. Hellenistic aestheticians, it is true, had increasingly associated art with beauty; but they were inconsistent, and they had trouble deciding which was more beautiful — nature or art.[8]

It is no surprise, therefore, when in another passage Plotinus takes up this very theme, considering the problem of whether art is more excellent than nature, and in a way more beautiful. In 5.8.1 Plotinus compares two blocks of stone. One is natural, the other a work of sculpture depicting a human being or a god. The sculpture, which obviously is not a representation of the rock it utilizes, and which in depicting a bodily form is also superior to any particular human body on earth, takes its idea from the artist. "The stone which has been brought to beauty of form by art will appear beautiful not because it is a stone (for then the other [stone] would be just as beautiful), but as a result of the form which art has put into it." Plotinus continues, with a distinctive emphasis of his own, "This beauty was in the art, and it was far better there; for the beauty in the art did not come into the stone: it stays in the art, and another comes from it into the stone which is derived from it and less than it" (5.8.1, trans. Armstrong, quoted in Tatarkiewicz, *Ancient Aesthetics*, p. 329).

Plotinus admits that one who is attuned to art will appreciate the

---

8. See Wladyslaw Tatarkiewicz, *Ancient Aesthetics*, vol. 1 of *History of Aesthetics*, 3 vols. (The Hague: Mouton, 1970), pp. 307, 295. The entire volume is an invaluable (if not always completely reliable) resource for the study of ancient aesthetics, containing extensive quotations in original languages as well as in English translation, and offering finely tuned analysis. Subsequent citations of this volume will be made parenthetically in the text.

beauty of the sculpture, just as a true musician is moved by an audible melody. But the higher beauty is not to be seen in the stone, but in the invisible art of the artist, just as the higher music is actually inaudible. (See 2.9.16 and 4.3.12.) For the adept, "The vision in the temple and the communion are achieved not with the statue, but with the divinity itself. . . . Contemplation is not a spectacle, but another form of vision, namely ecstasy" (6.9.11, trans. Armstrong, quoted in Tatarkiewicz, *Ancient Aesthetics,* p. 331).

Art, then, can be superior to nature. But that is because art has a more direct connection to the invisible form, to intellectual beauty, and possibly to the divine: "If anyone despises the arts because they produce their works by imitating nature, we must tell him, first, that natural things are imitations too: and then he must know that the arts do not simply imitate what they see; they go back to the *logoi* [ideas] from which nature derives; . . . since they possess beauty, they make up what is defective in things" (5.8.1, trans. Armstrong, quoted in Tatarkiewicz, *Ancient Aesthetics,* p. 328). In so praising art as an improvement on nature, Plotinus is implicitly distancing himself at this point from his avowed master, Plato, who criticized painting as a distant imitation of the real.

But in another respect Plotinus in his theory of art is at least as abstemious as Plato himself. Plotinus acknowledges that "beauty addresses itself chiefly to sight," and that there is also beauty of words and of musical melodies (1.6.1, trans. MacKenna, *Plotinus*). But he states repeatedly, and in many different ways, that "minds that lift themselves above the realm of sense to a higher order are aware of beauty in the conduct of life, in actions, in character, in the pursuits of the intellect; and there is the beauty of the virtues" (1.6.1, trans. MacKenna). Where does all this other beauty come from? It comes, as Plotinus is fond of pointing out, from the One, through the forms of intellect (related to Plato's "ideas") and the activity of embodied soul.

In what does any or all of this beauty consist, however? What lures sight and fills the eyes with joy at the sight? (1.6.1). For centuries, most of the Greek and Roman world would have answered that beauty is beheld in symmetry and in the harmony of parts, or proportion; and secondarily, perhaps, in graceful and colorful representation, or in charming or moving representation *(mimesis)*. But Plotinus reminds us that something that is symmetrical or well-proportioned must be made of parts. And that, he argues, counts against symmetry as essential to beauty. For if beauty were essentially tied to multiplicity, it would then be seen only in compounds. But in that case the single, individual parts could not be beautiful themselves; nor could individual colors or individual musical tones. Nor, indeed, could someone's character or conduct or a moral virtue (1.6.1). It is true, he admits, that good proportions are usually beautiful, but what makes them so is not the relation between the many elements but the soul that they manifest together, and thus the unity of the parts (6.7.22). We therefore have a parallel here to what Plotinus said about the higher beauty as existing in the art that makes the sculpture, not in the sculpture itself. Such an art has no "parts," but it derives from intellect and manifests soul and the quality of unity, which shows up in the sculpture.

Why doesn't Plotinus take a simpler, more obvious approach and conclude that there are various kinds of beauty, and correspondingly various ways in which something can be beautiful? That he studiously avoids any such notion suggests that he may have a hidden agenda in defining beauty in such a way — in saying that the essence of beauty is one thing only and that it is never, fundamentally, what one sees or hears, never really dependent on any sensuous perception or imagination, but is instead something alive, soul-ful, imperceptible, but nonetheless unified. Such a unitary but relatively disembodied notion of beauty fits with the larger "religious" aims of Plotinus, because it readily leads us away from sensible beauty toward intellectual beauty, and ultimately from the many to the One. There is never any doubt, in the *Enneads,* that the spiritual discipline of seeing that interests Plotinus most of all is one that ends up as quickly as possible in the image-less realm of pure, intellectual vision, a sense-less though blissful "perception" of invisible, timeless beauty.

Someone familiar with the aesthetics of Augustine, or with Advaita Vedanta in Hindu philosophy, or indeed with many modes of meditation in Buddhism, will recognize their affinity with the ultimately image-less "vision" in which the higher reaches of Plotinus's path culminates. The profundity of such approaches is hardly in doubt. But they may describe only one approach to the heights. What Plotinus and his counterparts typically rule out are alternative and perhaps equally beautiful ways of conceiving a spiritual path, in which art might play a central role. One wonders, in particular, if there is not an alternative that might honor sensory and artistic beauty in a more thoroughgoing manner — which a Christian might call sacramental. Perhaps there is a way to treat with greater love and appreciation the huge diversity of beauties, the individuality of beautiful beings, and the distinctive and different qualities of the many things in which we can find both aesthetic and religious value.

We will return to that possibility. For the moment, we need to round out our discussion of Plotinus's own views of art and beauty with the observation that Plotinus gives no clear indication as to what actually justifies calling both a visible painting of Zeus and an invisible virtue or intellectual pursuit "beautiful." He complains that a notion of beauty that is based on proportion can't account for the beauty of virtuous acts, since such acts are not amenable to measurement and therefore have no proportions. But if, as Plotinus seems to propose, the link between the beauty of a painting and the beauty of a virtue is their unity rather than good proportion, the problem does not disappear. For in what, or by what, is a given virtue "unified"? We can say that it is unified by being the thing it is; that is why it has an identity. But is the mere possession of an identity any reason to be considered beautiful — let alone more beautiful, or less beautiful, than something else? What does the word *beauty* add that the word *unity* lacks? If it adds merely the notion of being desirable, the same could be said of anything that is good (as Plotinus acknowledges). Why add the attribute "beautiful" to a good deed, if it has no specifiable aesthetic features? Moreover, if the beauty of a physical temple is not in some sense greater than — or at least valuable in a different way from — the beauty of the idea of a temple, then it is hard to see what one gains in terms of beauty by building or sculpting anything at all. Indeed, in that case it seems that the temple would be useless for anyone spiritually advanced — which is exactly what Plotinus implies, what various Christians have believed, and what certain Hindu teachers have proclaimed.

That brings us back to our question: Is there any better way, while drawing on Plotinus, to show or at least glimpse a more integral and reciprocal relationship between being beautifully artistic and being religious (or practicing religion in worship)?

Art as Spiritual Embodiment

With sufficient imagination we might be able to go back to bodily beauty itself and see how such beauty could contribute something distinctive to the life of the spirit. We could thus try to revise Plotinus for our time by attributing some distinctive spiritual merit to calisthenics and other aesthetic aspects of body training. But finding spiritual meaning in bodily beauty has hazards in a social context in which the movie star Halle Berry, in defending the pop singer Britney Spears against the charge that she is "too sexy," can declare bluntly (if reductively), "That's what [real] women are."[9]

Instead of taking on the whole complex issue of sex, gender, and beauty, it may be easier to revise Plotinus in a different way — by modifying his interpretation of the spiritual value of beautiful art. In the present context I must be content with doing so in terms of a single analogy.

Plotinus, in a well-known passage, likens the universe to a musical dance whose choir is under the direction of the great, divine Conductor:

> In the order of its singing the choir keeps round the conductor but may sometimes turn away, so that he is out of their sight, but when it turns back to him it sings beautifully and is truly with him; so we too are always around him — and if we were not, we should be totally dissolved and no longer exist — but not always turned to him; but when we do look to him, then we are at our goal and at rest and do not sing out of tune as we truly dance our god-inspired dance around him. (6.9.9, trans. Miles, *Plotinus*)

9. As reported on "Entertainment Weekly AOL," August 27, 2003.

In this analogy, which compares the most beautiful existence to the art of singing and dancing (closely related arts in antiquity), it is clear that nothing harmonious would be possible without the divine Conductor. Because this is an analogy, however, the reader must deduce where actual, earthly art as we know it — the art of music or dance or architecture — would fit into the scheme. As we have already seen, Plotinus suggests in many places that there is something special about the beauty of art, which speaks to soul and which brings to mind something of that cosmic dance and inaudible music. What he does not say is that some kind of spiritual discipline might consist in learning to attend to visible art and audible music in such a way that, more and more, one sees the depths of beautiful, sacred reality *in* the art and increasingly hears the heights of beautiful, sacred reality *in* the audible music.

Plotinus does not say that; but *we* could say that — especially in view of the fact that Plotinus has already prepared us to see with "soul" a kind of beauty in art and nature that is not strictly physical. Suppose that, contrary to what Plotinus usually says, the embodiment of soul in art's beauty is a creative act that makes for new possibilities not foreseen by soul or intellect — a common testimony of artists and art-lovers alike. Then it might turn out that a spiritual attentiveness to sensible forms and to aesthetically embodied imagination would itself be a spiritual discipline capable of great heights.

It is true that one cannot literally see the connection between the beauty we ascribe to sensuous art and the beauty we ascribe (for instance) to moral acts or invisible spiritual realities. But that is already a problem for Plotinus, or for anyone who would apply the term *beauty* (even by way of analogy) to something imperceptible. The problem is already well-known to us in discussing the arts, and it is one we live with all the time. Why do we call a poem beautiful or a story aesthetically engaging? It is only partly because of what we can literally perceive with our senses — the sound of the words, for instance. In larger part it is because the effect of the story or the poem engages our imaginations and senses in a total way that shares a close affinity with aesthetic response to art in its more sensuous and perceptible forms. We thus "perceive" a continuity between beauty as imagined or conceived mentally and beauty as perceived through the senses. Likewise, we "perceive" a continuity or analogy between the less embodied senses of divine presence (for instance) and the sense of the divine induced by a particular work of audible music, the very hearing of which may "sound" ineffably of the spirit.

Spiritual beauty as perceived in a work of music or in the architecture of a temple or Byzantine church could thus be experienced in different ways, depending on different dispositions and the differences in perceptible forms. Subjective and contextual differences need not rule out the reality of some greater beauty or beauties toward which the more subjective responses are likewise attuned, albeit in different ways. In this way there would be varieties of beauty, and a great good that derives from that very variety.

This would provide multiple ways for beauty to be delightful. Indeed, some beauty could well be a more "secular" sort that one might enjoy while looking briefly away from the cosmic Conductor, as it were. (Plotinus assures us that the conductor is always there; why would we need always to be looking directly?) That "looking away" in secular artistry and in relatively autonomous art could be part of the playfulness of art and religion both — not fearing that God jealously requires created beings to give the Conductor exclusive and direct attention, which is impossible for them in any case. We might even discover that looking at other people and objects is how we human beings often "see" best that One who is invisibly among us. That is to say, perhaps we connect with the divine by attending, in part, to the particular delights and moving tensions of the whole varied range of art, and of other beings, including those of nature. As Hildegard of Bingen said she heard God say in one of her revelations, "I am that living and fiery essence of the divine substance that glows in the beauty of the fields. I shine in the water, I burn in the sun and the moon and the stars."[10]

10. Hildegard of Bingen, quoted in Umberto Eco, *Art and Beauty in the Middle Ages,* trans. Hugh Bredin (New Haven, Conn.: Yale University Press, 1986), p. 47.

In modifying Plotinus in the way proposed above, we are recognizing a potential within earthly artistry and beauty that he hinted at, but in other ways questioned or undercut. Above all, we make it plain that we do not always need to turn away from sensible music and visible dance in order to ascend higher, even in a specifically religious sense. That is because Plotinus told a deeper truth than he realized when he said that visible earthly temples (or audible music or bodily dance) can be formed in such a way as to attract divinity (metaphorically speaking) and can enhance the embodied soul's sense of what is spiritual about beauty itself. The soul of us does not already know it all. It discovers more from actually making and beholding beautiful artistic forms. For the kinds of creatures that we are, that too is a way of our becoming "sun-like" and "god-like."

From a Christian point of view, at least, that spiritually disciplined way of making music and of partaking bodily in beauty may be an integral part of our participating in the sacred, cosmic dance of a sacramental universe. As John of Damascus wrote in defense of icons, "Perhaps you [iconoclasts] are sublime and able to transcend what is material . . . but I, since I am a human being and bear a body, want to deal with holy things and behold them in a bodily manner."[11] In seeing how the arts can participate in that bodily process of dealing with beautiful holy things, we likewise see how artistry and worship, while by no means identical, are (or should be) closely allied, and at times inseparable.

---

11. John of Damascus, quoted in Jaroslav Pelikan, *The Christian Tradition*, vol. 2: *The Spirit of Eastern Christendom (600-1700)* (Chicago: University of Chicago Press, 1974), p. 122.

Index

Adams, James Luther, 84n.26
Adams, John (composer), 58, 75
Aeschylus, 77
Aesthetics, xv-xvi, xvii, 132-33, 135;
Asian, 75-76, 143, 146, 148; judgments and taste in, 9-10, 12-25, 26-
29, 38-42, 46, 49-50, 51, 56, 60-62,
65-88 *passim*, 96-98, 143. *See also*
Arts; Beauty; Discernment
Alter, Robert, 52n.5
Aquinas, Thomas, 40, 119, 120, 133,
134
Aristotle, 134
Arts: attitudes toward, 12-25; diversity within religious, 3, 47-62, 65-
88 *passim*, 90, 96-98, 132-33, 135,
143; and faith, xv, 52-53, 78-80, 86-
88, 119, 121, 126, 151; good and
bad, 63-88; sacred and secular
styles of, 10, 24-25, 30-35, 42, 43-45,
94-98, 99, 101-2, 104-8, 109-13. *See
also* Aesthetics; Beauty; Music
Augustine, 40, 68, 102, 107-8, 119,
133, 139, 146

Bach, Johann Sebastian, 13, 41, 44,
58, 71, 78-79, 108, 113

Baker, Henry Williams, 92
Balthasar, Hans Urs von, 119, 133,
135n.6
Barth, Karl, 10, 14, 16, 39, 41, 44, 58,
113
Beauty, 10, 14, 16, 39, 49-50, 71, 84-
85, 86, 113, 118, 121, 123, 129-51. *See
also* Aesthetics; Arts
Beethoven, Ludwig von, 55, 56
Benedict XVI, 23, 80, 114-28
Berry, Halle, 148
Bible, 8-9, 10, 22, 26, 46, 48, 51, 52,
54, 90-98, 105, 119, 134
Billings, William, 40
Blankenburg, Walter, 104n.14,
106n.18, 108
Blume, Friedrich, 104n.14
Bonhoeffer, Dietrich, 85
Borg, Marcus, 85-86, 112
Bourdieu, Pierre, 18n.13
Bourgeois, Louis, 109
Britten, Benjamin, 75
Brown, Dan, 64
Bucer, Martin, 107, 108
Buddhism, 143
Budick, Sanford, 48
Butcher, Samuel, 70

Index